ISBN 978-1-331-55156-0
PIBN 10204835

1 MONTH OF
FREE
READING

at

www.ForgottenBooks.com

By purchasing this book you are eligible for one month membership to ForgottenBooks.com, giving you unlimited access to our entire collection of over 700,000 titles via our web site and mobile apps.

To claim your free month visit:
www.forgottenbooks.com/free204835

THE GREAT NORTH ROAD

HISTORIES OF THE ROADS

— BY —

CHARLES G. HARPER.

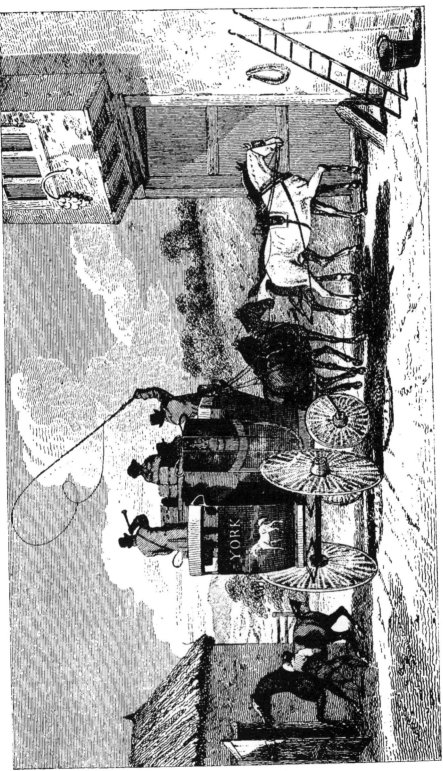

THE "HIGHFLYER," 1812.

After Emery.

The
GREAT NORTH ROAD

The Old Mail Road to Scotland

By CHARLES G. HARPER

YORK TO EDINBURGH

*With 77 Illustrations by the Author, and from
old-time Prints and Pictures*

LONDON :
CECIL PALMER
OAKLEY HOUSE, BLOOMSBURY STREET, W.C. 1

First Published in 1901.

Second and Revised Edition - 1922.

Printed in Great Britain by C. TINLING & Co.
53, Victoria Street, Liverpool.
Also at London and Prescot.

THE GREAT NORTH ROAD

YORK TO EDINBURGH

London (General Post Office) to—   MILES

	MILES
York	196¾
Clifton.	198¼
Rawcliff	200¼
Skelton	201¼
Shipton	202¾
Tollerton Lanes	206½
Easingwold	210¼
White House	211¾
Thormanby	214¼
Birdforth	215
Bagby Common (" Griffin " Inn) . . .	217½
Mile House	218½
Thirsk	220½
South Kilvington	222
Thornton-le-Street	223½
Thornton-le-Moor	224¾
Northallerton	229¼
Lovesome Hill	229¾
Little Smeaton (cross River Wiske). . .	231¾
Great Smeaton	232¾
High Entercommon	233¾
Dalton-on-Tees	236¾
Croft (cross River Tees) . . .	237¾
Oxneyfield Bridge (cross River Skerne) . .	238
Darlington	241¾
Harrowgate	243½

THE GREAT NORTH ROAD

	MILES
Coatham Mundeville	245¾
Aycliffe	246¾
Traveller's Rest	248
Woodham	249¼
Rushyford Bridge	250½
Ferryhill	253
Low Butcher Race and Croxdale . . .	255
Sunderland Bridge	255¾
Browney Bridge (cross River Wear)	256
Durham (cross River Browney) .	260
Durham Moor (Framwellgate) . . .	261
Plawsworth	263½
Chester-le-Street	266
Birtley	269
Gateshead Fell	271
Gateshead (cross River Tyne). . . .	273½
Newcastle-on-Tyne	274½
Gosforth	277
Seaton Burn	280¾
Stannington Bridge (cross River Blyth)	284
Stannington	284½
Clifton.	286½
Morpeth (cross River Wansbeck) . . .	289¼
Warrener's House	291¼
Priest's Bridge	293¼
West Thirston (cross River Coquet)	299¼
Felton	299¾
Newton-on-the Moor	302½
Alnwick (cross River Aln) . . .	308½
Heiferlaw Bank	310
North Charlton	314¾
Warenford	318¾
Belford	323
Detchant Cottages	325¼
Fenwick	328

MILEAGES.

	MILES
Haggerston	331
Tweedmouth (cross River Tweed) . . .	337½
Berwick-on-Tweed	338
Lamberton Toll	341

(ENTER SCOTLAND)

Greystonelees	343½
Flemington Inn and Burnmouth (cross River Eye)	344
Ayton	346
Houndwood	351¾
Grant's House	354½
Cockburnspath	358
Dunglass Dene	359¼
Broxburn	363½
Dunbar	365
Belhaven	365¾
Beltonford	367½
Phantassie	370
East Linton	370½
Haddington	376
Gladsmuir	379¾
Macmerry	381½
Tranent	383¼
Musselburgh (cross North Esk River)	387¼
Joppa	389¼
Portobello	390
Jock's Lodge	391½
Edinburgh	393

Via FERRYBRIDGE, WETHERBY, AND BOROUGHBRIDGE.

Doncaster (cross River Don) . . .	162¼
York Bar	164
Red House	167¼

THE GREAT NORTH ROAD

	MILES
Robin Hood's Well	169¼
Went Bridge (cross River Went)	172¾
Darrington	174½
Ferrybridge (cross River Aire)	177½
Brotherton	178½
Fairburn	180
Micklefield	184
Aberford	186½
Bramham Moor	189
Bramham	190¼
Wetherby (cross River Wharfe)	194¼
Kirk Deighton	195¼
Walshford Bridge (cross River Nidd)	197¼
Allerton Park	200¾
Nineveh	202½
Ornham's Hall	204¼
Boroughbridge (cross River Ure)	206¼
Kirkby Hill	207¼
Dishforth	210½
Asenby	212¼
Topcliffe (cross River Swale)	212¾
Sand Hutton	217
Newsham	219
South Otterington	220¾
North Otterington	222¼
Northallerton	225¼
Edinburgh	389

LIST OF ILLUSTRATIONS

THE GREAT NORTH ROAD

LIST OF ILLUSTRATIONS

THE GREAT NORTH ROAD

YORK TO EDINBURGH

I

AT last we are safely arrived at York, perhaps no cause for comment in these days, but a circumstance which "once upon a time" might almost have warranted a special service of prayer and praise in the Minster. One comes to York as the capital of a country, rather than of a county, for it is a city that seems in more than one sense Metropolitan. Indeed, you cannot travel close upon two hundred miles, even in England and in these days of swift communication, without feeling the need of some dominating city, to act partly as a seat of civil and ecclesiastical government, and partly as a distributing centre; and if something of this need is even yet apparent, how much more keenly it must have been felt in those " good old days " which were really so bad! A half-way house, so to speak, between those other capitals of London and Edinburgh, York had all the appearance of a capital in days of old, and has lost but little of it, in these,

B   1

even though in point of wealth and population it lags behind those rich and dirty neighbours, Leeds and Bradford. For one thing, it has a history to which they cannot lay claim, and keeps a firm hold upon titles and dignities conferred ages ago. We may ransack the pages of historians in vain in attempting to find the beginnings of York. Before history began it existed, and just because it seems a shocking thing to the well-ordered historical mind that the first founding of a city should go back beyond history or tradition, Geoffrey of Monmouth and other equally unveracious chroniclers have obligingly given precise—and quite untrustworthy—accounts of how it arose, at the bidding of kings who never had an existence outside their fertile brains.

When the Romans came, under Agricola, in A.D. 70, York was here. We do not know by what name the Brigantes, the warlike tribe who inhabited the northern districts of Britain, called it, but they possessed forts at this strategic point, the confluence of the rivers Ouse and Foss, where York still stands, and evidently had the military virtues fully developed, because it has seemed good to all who have come after them, from the Romans and the Normans to ourselves, to build and retain castles on the same sites. The Brigantes were a great people, despite the fact that they had no literature, no science, and no clothes with which to cover their nakedness, and were they in existence now, might be useful in teaching our War Office and commanding officers something of strategy and fortification. They have left memorials of their existence in the names of many places beginning with " Brig," and they are the sponsors of all the brigands that ever existed, for their name was a Brito-Welsh word meaning " hill-men " or " highlanders," and, as in the old days, to be a highlander was to be a thief and cut-throat, the chain of derivative facts that connects them with the bandits of two thousand years is complete.

A hundred and twenty years or so after the Romans had captured the Brigantes' settlement here, we find York suddenly emerging, a fully-fledged Roman city, from the prehistoric void, under the name of Eboracum. This was in the time of the Emperor Septimus Severus, who died in A.D. 211 in this *Altera Roma*, the principal city of Roman Britain. For this much is certain, that, as Winchester was, and London is, the capital of England, so was York at one time the chief city of the Roman colony, the foremost place of arms, of ru'e, and of residence ; and so it remained until Honorius, the hard-pressed, freed Britain from its allegiance in A.D. 410 and withdrew the legionaries. Two hundred years is a considerable length of time, even in the history of a nation, and much happened in Eboracum in that while. Another Roman emperor died here, in the person of Constantius Chlorus, and his son, Constantine the Great, whom some will have it was even born here, succeeded him. Both warred with the Pictish tribes from the North ; that inhospitable North which swallowed up whole detachments ; the North which Hadrian had conquered over two hundred years before, and now was exhausting the energies of the conquerors. Empire is costly in lives and treasure, and the tragedy of Roman conquest and occupation is even now made manifest in the memorials unearthed by antiquaries, recording the deaths of many of the Roman centurions at early ages. Natives of sunny Italy or of the south of France, they perished in the bleak hills and by the wintry rivers of Northumbria, much more frequently than they did at the hands of the hostile natives, who soon overwhelmed the magnificence of Eboracum when the garrisons left. The civilisation that had been established here, certainly since the time of Severus, was instantly destroyed, and Caer Evrauc, as it came to be called, became a heap of ruins. Then came the Saxons, who remodelled the name into Eoferwic, succeeded in turn by the Danes, from whose " Jorvic," pronounced with the soft J, we obtain Yorvic, the " Euerwic " of Domesday Book, and finally York. But whence the original " Eboracum " derived or what it meant is purely conjectural.

Christianity, fulfilling Divine promise, had brought " not peace, but a sword " to the Romans, and the Saxon king, Edwin of Northumbria, had not long been converted and baptized at York, on the site of the present Minster, before he was slain in conflict with the heathen. It was Paulinus, first Archbishop of York, who had baptized Edwin in 625. Sent to the North of England by Gregory the Great, as Augustine had already been sent for the conversion of the South, it was the Pope's intention to establish two Archbishoprics ; and thence arose centuries of quarrelling between the Archbishops of Canterbury and those of York as to who was supreme. York, indeed, only claimed equal rights ; but Canterbury claimed precedence. In the Synod of 1072 the Archbishop of York was declared subordinate to Canterbury, but half a century later, in order to make peace, Rome adjudged them equal. Even this did not still the strife, and Roger Pont l'Évêque, the Archbishop of York, who was contemporary with Becket, and aided the king in his struggle with that prelate, was especially bitter in the attempt to assert in a'l places and at all seasons this equality. He renewed the contention with Becket's successor, and provoked an absurd scene at the Council of Westminster in 1176, when, arriving late and finding the Archbishop of Canterbury present and already seated, he sat down in his lap. The result was that the Council of Westminster ·immediately resolved itself into a faction fight, in which my lord of York was jumped upon and kicked, for all the world like a football umpire who has given an unpopular decision. Even this did not settle either the Archbishop of York or the strife, and so at last, in 1354, it was decreed that each should be supreme in his own Province, and that the Archbishop of Canterbury should be " Primate of All England," while his brother of York should bear the title of "Primate of England"; but whenever an Archbishop of York was consecrated he should send to the Primate of All England a golden jewel, valued at £40, to be laid on the Shrine of St. Thomas "Thus," says Fuller, in his inimitably humorous manner, "when two children cry for the same apple, the indulgent father divides it between them, yet so that he gives the better part to the child which is his darling." Rome has long since ceased to have part or lot in the English Church, but this solemn farce of nomenclature is still retained.

In such things as these does York retain something of its old pride of place. Even its Mayor is a *Lord* Mayor, which was something to be proud of before these latter days, now Lord Mayors are three a penny, and every bumptious modern overgrown town is in process of obtaining one. The first Lord Mayor of York, however, was appointed by Richard the Second, and thus the title has an honourable antiquity.

In its outward aspect, York is varied. It runs the whole gamut, from the highest antiquity to the most modern of shops and villas ; from the neatest and tidiest streets to the most draggle-tailed and out-at-elbowed courts and alleys. From Clifton and Knavesmire, which is a great deal more respectable and clean than its evil-sounding name would lead the stranger to suppose, to the Shambles, Fossgate, and Mucky Peg's Lane (now purged of offence as Finkle Street) is a further social than geographical cry, and they certainly touch both extremes. "Mucky Peg" and the knaves of the waste lands outside the city are as historic in their way as Roman York, which lies nine feet below the present level of the streets, and for whose scanty relics one must visit the Museum of the Philosophical Society in the grounds of the ruined St. Mary's Abbey. In those grounds also the only fragment of the Roman walls may be seen, in the lower stage of the Multangular Tower, once commanding the bank of the river Ouse.

York is perhaps of all English towns and cities the

most difficult place to explore. Its streets branch and wind in every direction, without any apparent plan or purpose, and thus an exploration of the Walls, of which the city is, with reason, extremely proud, becomes the best means of ascertaining its importance and the relative positions of Castle and Minster. It is no short stroll, for, by the time the whole circuit is made, a distance of nearly three miles has been covered. These mediæval walls form, indeed, the most delightful promenade imaginable, being built on a grassy rampart and provided with a paved footpath running on the inner side of the battlements, and thus commanding panoramic

OLD YORK: THE SHAMBLES.

views within and without the city. Endeavour, by an effort of the imagination, to see the ground outside the walls free from the suburbs that now spread far in almost every direction, and you have the York of ancient days, little changed ; for from this point of view, looking down upon the clustered red roofs of the city, with its gardens and orchards, the towering bulk of the Minster, and the broad expanse of adjoining lawns, nearly all the signs of modern life are hidden. Something of an effort it is to imagine the great railway station of York away, for it bulks very largely outside the walls near the Lendal Bridge ; but the mediæval gates of the city help the illusion, and hint at the importance of the place in those times. Micklegate Bar, the chief of them, still bears the heraldic shields sculptured hundreds of years ago, when kings of England claimed also to be kings of France and quartered the *semée* of lilies with the lions. There are four arches now to this and three to the other bars, instead of but the one through which both pedestrian and other traffic went in olden times ; but the side arches have been so skilfully constructed in the mediæval style that they are not an offence, and are often, indeed, taken on trust as old by those unlearned in these things. Stone effigies of men-at-arms still appear on the battlemented turrets, and take on threatening aspects as seen against the skyline by approaching travellers. But did they ever achieve their purpose and succeed in deceiving an enemy into the belief that they were really flesh and blood ? If so, they must in those days have been very credulous folk, to be imposed upon by such devices.

Crossing the Ouse by Lendal Bridge, where chains stretched across the river from towers on either bank formerly completed the circle of defences, Bootham Bar is reached, spanning the exit from York along the Great North Road. Still a worthy approach to, or exit from, the city, it wore a yet more imposing appearance until towards the close of the coaching age, when its barbican, the outworks with which every one of the York bars was provided, was wantonly destroyed. Those who would recall the ancient appearance of Bootham Bar and its fellows, as viewed from without, have only to see Walmgate Bar, whose barbican still remains, the only one left in the march of intellect and of " improvements." Then it presented a forbidding front to the North, and with the walls, which were here at their highest and strongest, disputed the path of the Scots. The walls have been broken down and demolished between the river and this bar, and modern streets driven through, so that something of the grim problem presented to a northern enemy is lost to the modern beholder ; but the view remains among the finest, and comprises the towers of the Minster, peering in grandeur from behind this warlike frontal. The Scots were here soon after Bannockburn. In 1319 an army of 15,000 came down, and York would probably have fallen had it not been for these strong defences, the finest examples of military architecture in England. As it was, they found York too well cared for, and so, destroying everything outside the walls and leaving it on their left, they endeavoured to pass south by Ferrybridge. At Myton-upon-Swale, near Borough-bridge, they met the English, hastily brought up by the Archbishop, and defeated them with the utmost ease. But prudence was ever a Scottish characteristic, and so, with much booty, they retreated into Scotland, instead of following up their advantage.

The walk along the walls from Bootham Bar to Monk Bar is glorious in spring, with the pink and white blossoms of apple, pear, and plum-trees, for here the well-ordered gardens of the ecclesiastical dignitaries are chiefly situated. Midway, the wall makes a return in a south-easterly direction. Monk Bar, whose name derives from General Monk, Duke of Albemarle, was once known as Goodramgate, and the street in which it stands still bears that name, supposed to be a corruption of " Guthram," the name of some forgotten Danish chieftain. At some distance beyond it, the wall goes off due east, to touch the river Foss at Layerthorpe, where that stream and the quagmires that once bordered it afforded an excellent defence in themselves, without any artificial works. Thus it is that the wall ceases entirely until the Red Tower is reached, on the

THE WALLS OF YORK.

outer bank of the Foss, where it recommences and takes a bend to the south-west. From this point to Walmgate Bar and the Fishergate Postern it is particularly slight, the necessary strength being provided by the Foss itself, forming a second line of defence, with the castle behind it. Thence we come to the broad Ouse again, now crossed by the Skeldergate Bridge, but once protected, as at Lendal, by chains drawn from bank to bank. On the opposite bank, on the partly natural elevation of Baile Hill, stood a subsidiary castle, and here the wall is carried on a very high mound until it rejoins Micklegate Bar.

There are but few so-called " streets " in York. They are mostly " gates," a peculiarity of description which is noticeable throughout the Midlands and the North. And queerly named some of these " gates " are. There is Jubbergate, whose name perpetuates the memory of an ancient Jewish quarter established here ; Stonegate, the narrow lane leading to the Minster, along which went the stone with which to build it ; Swinegate, a neighbourhood where the unclean beasts were kept, and many more. But most curious of all is " Whipmawhopmagate," a continuation of Colliergate. This oddly named place is rarely brought to the notice of the stranger, because it has but two houses ; but, despite its whimsical name, it has a real, and indeed a very old, existence. Connected with its name is the institution of " Whip Dog Day," a celebration once honoured on every St. Luke's Day, October 18, by the thrashing of all the dogs met with in the city. According to the legend still current, it seems that in mediæval times, while the priest was celebrating the sacrament at the neighbouring church of St. Crux, he dropped the consecrated pax, which was swallowed by a stray dog who had found his way into the building. For this crime the animal was sentenced to be severely whipped, and an annual day was set apart for the indiscriminate thrashing of his fellows. A more likely derivation of the name of Whipmawhopmagate is from the spot having been the whipping-place of religious penitents, or of merely secular misdemeanants.

II

THE grim blackened walls of York Castle confront the traveller who approaches the city by Fishergate, and lend a gloomy air to the entrance ; the more gloomy because those heavy piles of sooty masonry nowadays encircle a prison for malefactors, rather than forming the defences of a garrison, and keep our social enemies within, instead of a more chivalric foe without. For over two hundred years York Castle has been an assize court and a gaol, and the military element no longer lends it pure romance. Romance of the sordid kind it has, this beetle-browed place of vain regrets and expiated crimes, of dismal cells and clanking fetters ; but if you would win back to the days of military glory which once distinguished it, your imaginary journey will be lengthy indeed. These battlemented walls, enclosing four acres of ground, and with a compass of over eleven hundred yards, were completed in 1856, and, with the prison arrangements within, cost £200,000. If, as the poet remarks, " peace hath her victories, no less renowned than war," she also needs defences, as much against the villainous centre-bit as against the foreign foe.

But there is still something left of the York Castle of old, although you must win to it past frowning portals eloquent of a thousand crimes, great and small, guarded by prison warders and decorated with notice-boards of Prison Regulations. Clifford's Tower, this ancient portion, itself goes no farther back into history than the time of Edward the First ; and of the buildings that witnessed the appalling massacre of the Jews, in March 1190, nothing fortunately remains. It cannot be to the advantage of sightseers that the blood-stained stones of that awful time should stand. History alone, without the aid of sword or shattered wall, is more than sufficient to keep the barbarous tale alive, of how some five hundred Jews of all ages and sexes fled for protection to the Castle keep, and were besieged there for days by Christians, thirsting for their blood. Their death was sure : only the manner of it remained uncertain. The wholesale slaughter of Jews at Lynn, Lincoln, and Stamford rendered surrender impossible, and rather than die slowly in the agonies of starvation they set the Castle on fire, husbands and brothers slaying the women and children, and then stabbing themselves. Those few who feared to die thus opened the gates as morning dawned. " Affliction has taught us wisdom," they said, " and we long for baptism and for the faith and peace of Christ " ; but even as they said it the swords and axes of ruthless assassins struck them down. Christ was avenged, and, incidentally, many a Christian debtor cried quits with his Jewish creditor as he dashed out the infidel's brains. It is not often given to champions of causes, religious or political, to make one blow serve both public and private ends, and those Christians were fortunate. At the same time, sympathy with the murdered Jews may easily be overstrained. They had but sown the wind and reaped the whirlwind. Trading and following the traditional Jewish occupation of usury, they had eaten like a canker into the heart of York. They had lived in princely style, and knew how to grind the faces of their Christian debtors, whose lives they had made miserable, and so simply fell victims to that revenge which has been aptly described as " a kind of wild justice."

Clifford's Tower, standing where these scenes were enacted, is a roofless shell, standing isolated on its mound within the Castle walls, and obtains its name, not from its builder, but from Francis Clifford, Earl of Cumberland, who made a doorway in it in the time of Charles the First. It was ruined by explosion and fire in 1684, and so remains, shattered and overgrown with trees and grass, a picturesque object that the eye loves to linger upon in contrast with the classic buildings that occupy the old Castle wards, and speak of crime and its penalties. He who would bring back the crimes and ferocities of a hundred and fifty years or more to the mind's eye can have his taste gratified

YORK CASTLE: CLIFFORD'S TOWER.

and the most vivid pictures conjured up at the sight of such choice and thrilling relics as the horn-handled knife and fork with which the bodies of rebels captured in the '45 were quartered; the leathern strap that Holroyd used for the purpose of hanging his father from the boughs of a cherry-tree; a fragment of the skull of Eugene Aram's victim, Daniel Clark; the curiously varied implements used by wives and husbands who murdered their yoke-fellows, ranging from the unwifely sledge-hammer and razor wielded by wives, to the knives and pokers chiefly affected by the husbands; Jonathan Martin the incendiary's impromptu flint and steel, and the bell rope by whose aid he escaped from the Minster; and those prime curiosities, Dick Turpin's fetters. Even Turpin's cell

can be seen by those who, after much diligent application to the Prisons Department of the Home Office,
procure the *entrée* to the Castle ; and in that " stone
jug," as the criminals of old called their cells, the
imaginative can reconstruct their Turpin as they will.
Many a better man than he has occupied this gloomy
dungeon, but scarce a worse.

III

ONE of the most notorious of the criminals who were
haled forth from this condemned hold to end their days
on Knavesmire was Richard Turpin, who was hanged on
the 17th of April, 1739.   This cruel and mean ruffian,
around whose sordid career the glamour of countless
legends of varying degrees of impossibility has gathered,
was the son of a small innkeeper and farmer at the
appropriately named village of Hempstead, in Essex.
The inn, called the " Crown," almost wholly rebuilt,
however, is in existence to this day, and his baptismal
record may yet be read in the parish register :—
" 1705, Sept. 21, *Richardus, filius Johannis et Mariae
Turpin.*"
Apprenticed to a butcher in Whitechapel, he soon
set up in business for himself, obtaining his cattle by
the simple and ready expedient of stealing them.
He married a girl named Palmer, whose name he
afterwards took, and after a career of house-breaking
and cattle-lifting in Essex and parts of Middlesex,
in which he figured as one of a numerous gang who
never attacked or plundered unless they were armed
to the teeth and in a great numerical superiority,
found the home counties too hot to hold him ; and
so, after shooting his friend, one of the three brothers
King, all highwaymen, in the affray at Whitechapel
in 1737, in which he escaped from the Bow Street
officers, he fled first into Essex and then into Lincolnshire.   Authorities disagree, both as to the particular

King who was shot, and on the question of whether
Turpin shot him accidentally in aiming at one of the
officers, or with the purpose of preventing him giving
evidence disclosing his haunts. The legends make
Tom King the martyr on this occasion, and represent
him as bidding Turpin to fly ; but the facts seem to
point to Matthew being the victim, and to his cursing
Turpin for a coward, as he died. It is quite certain
that *a* Tom King, a highwayman, suffered at Tyburn
in 1755, eight years later.

As for Turpin, or Palmer, as he now called himself,
he settled at Welton, near Beverley, and then at
Long Sutton, Lincolnshire, as a gentleman horse-dealer.
He had not long been domiciled in those parts before
the farmers and others began to lose their stock
in a most unaccountable manner. The wonder is that
no one suspected him, and that he could manage, for
however short a period, to safely sell the many horses he
stole. He even managed to mix freely in company
with the yeomen of the district, and despite his
ill-favoured countenance, made himself not unwelcome.
But his brutal nature was the cause of his undoing.
Returning from a shooting excursion, he wantonly
shot one of his neighbour's fowls, and on being
remonstrated with, threatened to serve one of his new
friends the same. He was accordingly summoned at
the Beverley Petty Sessions, when it appeared that he
had no friends to find bail for him, and that he was, in
point of fact, a newcomer to the district, whose habits,
now investigated for the first time, proved suspicious.
Eventually he was charged with stealing a black mare,
blind of the near eye, off Heckington Common, and was
committed to York Castle. From his dungeon cell he
wrote a letter to his brother at Hempstead, to cook
him up a character. The letter was not prepaid, and
the brother, not recognising the handwriting, refused
to pay the sixpence demanded by the Post Office. On
such trivial things do great issues hang ! The village
postmaster happened to have been the schoolmaster
who had taught Turpin to write. He recognised the

handwriting and read the letter. He was a man of public spirit, and, travelling to York, identified the prisoner as the Richard Turpin who had long been " wanted " for many crimes.

After his trial and condemnation the farmers flocked in hundreds to see him. His last days in prison were as well attended as a levee, and, to do him justice, his courage, conspicuously lacking at other times, never faltered at the last. He became one of the shows of that ancient city for a time, but nothing daunted him. He spent his last days in joking, drinking, and telling stories, as jovial, merry, and frolicsome as though the shadow of the gallows was not impending over him. He scouted the Ordinary, and suffered no twinges of conscience, but busied himself in preparing a decent costume for his last public appearance. Nothing would serve him but new clothes and a smart pair of pumps to die in. On the morning before the execution, he gave the hangman £3. 10s. to be divided among five men who were to follow him as mourners, and were to be furnished with black hatbands and mourning gloves. When the time came and he went in the tumbril to be turned off, he bowed to the ladies and flourished his cocked hat as though he would presently see them again. He certainly, when he had mounted the ladder, kept the people waiting for the spectacle they had come to see, for he talked with the hangman for over half-an-hour. But when the conversation was ended, he threw himself off in the most resolute fashion, and had the reward of his courage, for he died in a moment.

Thus died the famous Turpin, in the thirty-third year of his age. After the execution his body lay in state for that day and the succeeding night at the " Black Boar " inn in Castlegate. The following morning it was buried in the churchyard of St. George's, by Fishergate Postern, and the evening afterwards it was dug up again by some of the city surgeons, for dissection. By this time the mob had apparently agreed that this brutal horse-stealer, who according to the contemporary *London Magazine,* was " so mean and stupid a wretch," was really a very fine fellow ; and they determined that his remains should not be dishonoured. Accordingly they rescued the body and reinterred it, in black lime, so as to effectually balk any further attempts on the part of the surgeons.

Dick Turpin, although his name bulks so largely in the legendary story of the roads, was by no means the foremost of his profession. He was brutal, and lacked the finer instincts of the artist. It could never, for instance, have been in his nature to invite the wife of a traveller he had just robbed to dance a coranto with him on the Common, as Duval did on Hounslow Heath when the distant clocks were sounding the hour of midnight. With Turpin it was an oath and a blow. Curses and violence, not courtesy, were his methods. Therefore, it is with the less compunction that we may tear away the romance from Richard Turpin and say that, so far from being the hero of the Ride to York, he never rode to York at all, except on that fatal morning when he progressed to York Castle in chains, presently to be convicted and hanged for the unromantic crimes of horse, sheep, and cattle stealing. He was little better than a vulgar burglar and horse-thief. It was Harrison Ainsworth who made Turpin a hero from such very unpromising material, and he, in fact, invented not only the ride to York, but Black Bess as well. According to the novelist, Turpin started from Kilburn, and came into the Great North Road at Highgate, with three mounted officers after him. Thence he turned into Hornsey, and so by the Ware route, the mare clearing the twelve feet high toll-gate on the way without an effort. They always do that in fiction, but the animal that could do it in fact does not exist.

At Tottenham (always according to the novelist, of course) the people threw brickbats at the gallant Turpin. They " showered thick as hail, and quite as harmlessly, around him," and Turpin laughed, as, indeed, he had an occasion to do, because the Tottenham people must have been the poorest of marksmen. And so pursuers and pursued swept through Edmonton and Ware, and quite a number of places which are not on our route. At Alconbury Hill he comes into view again, and the inconceivable chase proceeds until Black Bess expires, at sunrise, within sight of the glorious panorama of York's spires and towers.

There are very many who believe Ainsworth's long rigmarole, and take their ideas of that unromantic highwayman from his novel, but the dashing, high-souled (and at times maudlin) fellow of those pages is absolutely fictitious.

IV

AINSWORTH constructed his fictitious hero from a very slight basis of fact. What a pity he did not rear his narrative on better lines, and give the credit of the Ride to York to the man who really did it. For it *was* done, and it was a longer ride by some twenty-six miles, at least, than that recounted in the vulgar romance of *Rookwood*. It was, in fact, a better ride, by a better man, and at a much earlier period.

John Nevison was the hero of this exploit. It was on a May morning in 1676, at the unconscionable hour of four o'clock, that he robbed a traveller on Gad's Hill, near Chatham, and, fired with the ambition of establishing an *alibi*, immediately set off to ride to York. Crossing the Thames from Gravesend to Tilbury, he rode on his " blood bay " to Chelmsford, where he baited and rested his horse for half-an-hour. Thence on to Cambridge and through the town without drawing rein, he went through by-lanes to Fenny Stanton, Godmanchester, and Huntingdon, where he took another half-hour's rest ; continuing, by unfrequented ways, until York was reached, the same evening. Of course, he must have had several fresh horses on the way. Stabling the horse that had brought

him into the cathedral city, he hastily removed the
travel-stains from his person, and strolled casually to
the nearest bowling-green, where the Mayor of York
happened to be playing a game with some friends.
Nevison took the opportunity of asking him the time,
and received the answer that it was just a quarter to
eight. That was sufficient for his purpose. By this
question and the reply he had fixed the recollection of
himself and of the time in the Mayor's mind, and had
his *alibi* at need. Sure enough, he needed it a little
later, when he was arrested for another highway
robbery, and the Gad's Hill traveller happened to be
the one witness who could swear to him. Nevison
called his York witnesses, who readily enough deposed
to his being there on the evening of the day on which
the traveller swore he had been robbed by him near
Chatham. This was conclusive. No one conceived
it possible for a man to have been in two places so
remote in one day, and he was acquitted. Then,
when the danger was past, his sporting instincts
prevailed, and he told the story. He became the hero
of a brief hour, and Charles the Second, who dearly
loved a clever rogue, is said to have christened him
" Swift Nicks." If we roughly analyse this ride we
shall find that Nevison's performance amounted to
about 230 miles in fifteen hours : a rate of over
fifteen miles an hour. To have done as much was a
wonderful exploit, even though (as seems certain) he
had remounts at the houses of confederates. He
probably had many such houses of call, for he was
one of a numerous band of highwaymen whose headquarters were at Newark.

This escape served him for eight years longer, for
it was in 1684 that his career came to a close on
Knavesmire, where he was hanged on the 4th of May.

There was something of the Robin Hood in Nevison's
character, if we are to believe the almost legendary
stories told in Yorkshire of this darling of the Yorkshire
peasantry. He robbed the rich and gave to the poor,
and many are the tales still told of his generosity.

Such an one is the tale that tells of his being at a village inn, when the talk turned upon the affairs of an unfortunate farmer whose home had been sold up for rent. Among those in the place was the bailiff, with the proceeds of the sale on him. Nevison contrived to relieve him of the cash, and restored it to the farmer. Perhaps he was not so well-liked by the cattle-dealers along the Great North Road, whom he and his gang robbed so regularly that at length they commuted their involuntary contributions for a quarterly allowance, which at the same time cleared the road for them and afforded them protection against any other bands. Indeed, Nevison, or Bracy, as his real name appears to have been, was in this respect almost a counterpart of those old German barons on the Rhine, who levied dues on the travellers whose business unfortunately led them their way. The parallel goes no greater distance, for those picturesque miscreants were anything but the idols of the people. Nevison was sufficiently popular to have been the hero of a rural ballad, still occasionally heard in the neighbourhood of his haunts at Knaresborough, Ferrybridge, York, or Newark. Here are two verses of it ; not perhaps distinguished by wealth of fancy or resourcefulness of rhyme :—

> Did you ever hear tell of that hero,
>   Bold Nevison, that was his name ?
> He rode about like a bold hero,
>   And with that he gain'd great fame.

> He maintained himself like a gentleman,
>   Besides, he was good to the poor ;
> He rode about like a great he o,
>   And he gain'd himself favour therefore.

Yorkshire will not willingly let the fame of her Nevison die. Is not his Leap shown, and is not the inn at Sandal, where he was last captured, still pointed out ? Then there is the tale of how he and twenty of his gang attacked fifteen butchers who were riding to Northallerton Fair, an encounter recounted in a pamphlet dated 1674, luridly styled *Bloody News from Yorkshire*. Another memory is of the half dozen men who at another time attempted to take him prisoner. He escaped and shot one of them, also a butcher. Nevison and butchers were evidently antipathetic. Released once on promising to enter the army, he, like Boulter, deserted. That he could break prison with the best he demonstrated fully at Wakefield ; but his final capture was on a trivial charge. It sufficed to do his business, though, for the prosecution were now prepared with the fullest evidence against him and his associates, and their way of life. They had secured Mary Brandon, who acted as housekeeper for the gang. According to her story, they were John Nevison, of York ; Edmund Bracy, of Nottingham ; Thomas Wilbere, of the same town ; Thomas Tankard, vaguely described as " of Lincolnshire " ; and two men named Bromett and Iverson. This last was " commonly at the ' Talbott,' in Newarke," which was their headquarters. The landlord of that inn was supposed to be cognisant of their doings, as also the ostler, one William Anwood, " shee haveinge often seene the said partyes give him good summs of money, and order him to keepe their horses close, and never to water them but in the night time." They kept rooms at the " Talbot " all the year round, and in them divided their spoil, which in one year, as the result of ten great robberies, came to over £1,500. No other highwaymen can hold a candle to this gang, either for their business-like habits or the success of their operations.

V

THAT once dreaded mid-eighteenth century highway-man, Thomas Boulter, junior, of Poulshot in Wiltshire, once made acquaintance with York Castle. The extent of his depredations was as wide as his indifference to danger was great. A West-countryman, his most obvious sphere of operations was the country through which the Exeter Road passed ; but being greedy and

insatiable, he soon exhausted those districts, and
thought it expedient to strike out for roads where the
name of Boulter was unknown, and along which the
lieges still dared to carry their watches and their gold.
He came up to town at the beginning of 1777 from his
haunts near Devizes, and, refitting in apparel and
pistols, gaily took the Great North Road. Many
adventures and much spoil fell to him in and about
Newark, Leeds, and Doncaster; but an encounter
between Sheffield and Ripon proved his undoing. He
had relieved a gentleman on horseback of purse and
jewellery, and was ambling negligently away when the
traveller's man-servant, who had fallen some distance
behind his master, came galloping up. Thus reinforced,
the plundered one chased Mr. Boulter, and, running
him to earth, haled him off to the nearest Justice,
who, quite unmoved by his story of being an unfortunate young man in the grocery line, appropriately
enough named Poore, committed him to York Castle,
where, at the March assizes, he was duly found guilty
and sentenced to be hanged within fifteen days.
Heavily ironed, escape was out of the question, and
he gave himself up for lost, until, on the morning
appointed for his execution, the news arrived that he
might claim a free pardon if he would enter his
Majesty's service as a soldier, and reform his life.
His Majesty badly wanted soldiers in A.D. 1777, and
was not nice as to the character of his recruits; and
indeed the British army until the close of the Peninsular
War was composed of as arrant a set of rascals as ever
wore out shoe-leather. No wonder the Duke of
Wellington spoke of his army in Spain as " my black-
guards." But they could fight.

This by the way. To return to Mr. Thomas Boulter,
who, full of moral resolutions and martial ardour, now
joined the first marching regiment halting at York.
For four days he toiled and strove in the barrack-yard,
finding with every hour the burdens of military life
growing heavier. On the fifth day he determined to
desert, and on the sixth put that determination into

practice ; for if he had waited until the morrow, when his uniform would have been ready, escape would have been difficult. Stealing forth at dead of night, without mishap, he made across country to Nottingham, and so disappears altogether from these pages. The further deeds that he did, and the story of his end are duly chronicled in the pages of the *Exeter Road,* to which they properly belong.

The authorities did well to secure their criminal prisoners with irons, because escape seems to have otherwise been easy enough. In 1761, for instance, there were a hundred and twenty-one French prisoners of war confined in York Castle, and such captives were of course not ironed. Some of them filed through the bars of their prison and twenty escaped. Of these, six were recaptured, but the rest were never again heard of, which seems to be proof that the prison was scarcely worthy of the name, and that the city of York contained traitors who secretly conveyed the fugitives away to the coast.

The troubles and escapades of military captives are all in the course of their career, and provoke interested sympathy but not compassion, because we know full well that they would do the same to their foes, did fortune give the opportunity. Altogether different was the position of the unfortunate old women who, ill-favoured or crazy, were charged on the evidence of ill-looks or silly talk with being witches, and thrown into the noisome cells that existed here for such. Theirs were sad cases, for the world took witchcraft seriously and burnt or strangled those alleged practitioners of it who had survived being " swum " in the river close by. The humour of that old method of trying an alleged witch was grimly sardonic. She was simply thrown into the water, and if she sank was innocent. If, on the other hand, she floated, that a was proof that Satan was protecting his own, and she was fished out and barbarously put to death. Trials for witchcraft were continued until long after the absurdity of the charges became apparent, and judges simply treated the accusations with humorous contempt : as when a crazy old woman who pretended to supernatural powers was brought before Judge Powell. " Do you say you can fly ? " asked the Judge, interposing. " Yes, I can," said she. " So you may, if you will then," rejoined that dry humorist. " I have no law against it." The accused did not respond to the invitation.

So farewell, grim Castle of York, old-time prison of such strangely assorted captives as religious pioneers, poor debtors, highwaymen, prisoners of war, and suspected witches ; and modern gaol whose romance is concealed beneath contemporary common-places. Blood stains your stones, and persecution is writ large on the page of your story. Infidel Jews, Protestants, Catholics, and Nonconformists of every shade of nonconformity have suffered within your walls in greater or less degree, and even now the black flag occasionally floats dolorously in the breeze from your roofs, in token that the penalty for the crime of Cain has been exacted.

VI

BEFORE railways came and rendered London the chief resort of fashion, county towns, and many lesser towns still, were social centres. Only the wealthier among the country squires and those interested in politics to the extent of having a seat in the House visited London ; the rest resorted to their county town, in which they had their town-houses and social circles. Those times are to be found reflected in the pages of Jane Austen and other early novelists, who picture for us the snug coteries that then flourished and the romances that ran their course within the unromantic-looking Georgian mansions now either occupied by local professional men or wealthy trades-folk, or else divided into tenements. It was the era before great suburbs began to spring up around

every considerable town, to smother the historic in
the commonplace ; the time before manufacturing
industries arose to smirch the countryside and to rot
the stonework of ancient buildings with smoke and
acid-laden air ; the days when life was less hurried
than now. York, two days' journey removed from
London, had its own society and a very varied one,
consisting of such elements as the Church, the Army,
and the Landed Interest, which last must also be
expressed in capital letters, because in those days to
be a Landowner was a patent of gentility. Outside
these elements, excepting the dubious ones of the
Legal and Medical professions, there was no society.
Trade rendered the keepers of second-hand clothes-
shops and wealthy manufacturers equally pariahs
and put them outside the pale of polite intercourse.
Society played whist in drawing-rooms ; tradesmen
played quoits, bowls, or skittles in grounds attached
to inns, or passed their evenings in convivial bar
parlours. Yet York must have been a noted place
for conviviality, if we are to believe the old poet :—

> York, York for my monie,
> Of all the cities that ever I see,
> For merry pastime and companie,
> Except the citie of London.

And for long after those lines were written they held
good. Not many other cities had York's advantages
as a great military headquarters, as well as the head
of an ecclesiastical Province, and its position as a great
coaching centre to and from which came and went
away many other coaches besides those which fared
the Great North Road was commanding. Cross-
country coach-routes radiated from the old cathedral
city in every direction ; just as, in fact, the railways
do nowadays. It is no part of our business to particu-
larise them, but the inns they frequented demand a
notice. Some of these inns were solely devoted to
posting, which in this broad-acred county of wealthy
squires was not considered the extravagance that less
fortunate folks thought it. Chief among these was—

alas ! that we must say *was*—the " George," which
stood almost exactly opposite the still extant " Black
Swan " in Coney Street.   A flaunting pile of business
premises occupied by a firm of drapers now usurps the
site of that extremely picturesque old house which
rejoiced in a sixteenth-century frontage, heavily
gabled and enriched with quaint designs in plaster, and
a yawning archway, supported on either side by
curious figures whose lower anatomy ended in scrolls,
after the manner of the Renaissance.   The " George "
for many years enjoyed an unexampled prosperity, and
the adjoining houses, of early Georgian date, with
projecting colonnade, were annexed to it.   When it
went, to make way for new buildings, York lost its
most picturesque inn, for the York Tavern, now
Harker's Hotel, though solid, comfortable, and pros-
perons-looking, with its cleanly stucco front, is not
interesting, and the " Black Swan " is a typical red-
brick building of two hundred years ago, square as a
box, and as little decorative as it could possibly be.
As for the aristocratic Etteridge's, which stood in
Lendal, it may be sought in vain in that largely rebuilt
quarter.   Etteridge's not only disdained the ordinary
coaching business, but also jibbed at the average
posting people—or, perhaps, to put it more correctly,
even the wealthy squires who flung away their money
on posting stood aghast at Etteridge's prices.   Therefore, in those days, when riches and gentility went
together—before the self-made millionaires had risen,
like scum, to the top—Etteridge's entertained the
most select, who travelled in their own " chariots,"
and were horsed on their almost royal progresses by
Etteridge and his like.

From the purely coaching point of view, the " Black
Swan " is the most interesting of York's hostelries.
To the York Tavern came the mails, while the " Black
Swan " did the bulk of the stage-coach business, from
the beginning of it in 1698 until the end, in 1842.   It
was here that the old " York in Four Days " coaching
bill of 1706 was discovered some years ago.   The house

remained one of the very few unaltered inns of coaching days, the stableyard the same as it was a hundred years or more since, even to the weather-beaten old painted oval sign of the " Black Swan," removed from the front and nailed over one of the stable-doors.

York still preserves memories of the old coachmen ; some of them very great in their day. Tom Holtby's, for instance, is a classic figure, and one that remained until long after coaching came to an end. He died in June 1863, in his seventy-second year, and was therefore, not greatly beyond his prime when he drove the Edinburgh mail into York for the last time, in 1842, on the opening of the railway. That last drive was an occasion not to be passed without due ceremony, and so when the mail, passing through Selby and Riccall, on its way to the city, reached Escrick Park, it was driven through, by Lord Wenlock's invitation, and accompanied by him on his drag up to the " Black Swan " and to the York Tavern. The mail flew a black flag from its roof, and Holtby gave up the reins to Lord Macdonald.

" Please to remember the coachman," said my lord to Holtby, in imitation of the professional's usual formula. " Yes," replied Holtby, " I will, if you'll remember the guard." " Right," said that innocent nobleman, not thinking for the moment that coach-men and guards shared their tips ; " he shall have double what you tip me." Holtby accordingly handed him a £5. note, so that he reaped a profit of £2. 10s. on the business.

Holtby's career was as varied as many of the old coachmen's, but more prosperous. He began as a stable-hand at the " Rose and Crown," Easingwold, and rose to be a postboy. Thence to the box of a cross-country coach was an easy transition, and his combined dash and certainty as a whip at last found him a place on the London and Edinburgh " High-flyer," whence he was transferred to the mail. During these years he had saved money, and was a compara-tively rich man when coaching ended ; so that although he lost some heavy sums in ill-judged investments, still he died worth over £3,000. " Rash Tom," as they called him, from his showy style of driving, was indeed something of a " Corinthian," and coming into contact with the high and mighty of that era, reflected their manners and shared their tastes. If the reflection, like that of a wavy mirror, was not quite perfect, and erred rather in the direction of caricature, that was a failing not found in Tom only, and was accordingly overlooked. Moreover, Tom was useful. No man could break in a horse like him, and nowhere was a better tutor in the art of driving. " If," said Old Jerry, " Tom Holtby didn't live on potato-skins and worn't such a one for lickin' folks' boots, he'd be perfect." " Old Jerry," who probably had some professional grudge against Holtby, referred to potato-skins as well as to boot-licking in a figurative way. He meant to satirise Holtby as a saving man and as an intimate of those who at the best treated Jerry himself with obvious condescension. Jerry himself was one of the most famous of postboys, and remained for long years in the service of the " Black Swan." The burden of his old age was the increasing meanness of the times. " Them wor graand toimes for oos ! " he would say, in his Yorkshire lingo, talking of the early years of the nineteenth century, and so they must have been, for that was the tail-end of the era when all England went mad over Parliamentary elections, and when Yorkshire, the biggest of all the counties, was the maddest. Everybody posted, money was spent like water on bribery and corruption, and on more reputable items of expenditure, and postboys shared in the golden shower.

VII

THE most exciting of these Homeric election contests was the fierce election for Yorkshire in 1807. At that time the huge county, larger than any other two

counties put together, returned only two representa-
tives to Parliament, and the City of York was the sole
voting-place. Yorkshire, roughly measuring eighty
miles from north to south, and another eighty from
east to west, must have contained ardent politicians
if its out-voters appeared at the poll in any strength.
But if polling-places were to seek and voting the
occasion of a weary pilgrimage, at least the authorities
could not be accused of allowing too little time for
the exercise of that political right. The booths
remained open for fifteen days. William Wilberforce
had for years been the senior member, and had hitherto
held a secure position. On this particular occasion
the contest lay between the rival houses of Fitzwilliam
and Lascelles, Whigs and Tories respectively, intent
upon capturing the junior seat. Lord Milton, the
eldest son of Earl Fitzwilliam, and the Honourable
Henry Lascelles, heir to the Earl of Harewood,
were the candidates. Lord Harewood expressed his
intention of expending, if necessary, the whole of his
Barbados estates, worth £40,000 a year, to secure his
son's return, and equal determination was shown by
the other side. With such opponents, it was little
wonder that Yorkshire was turned into a pandemonium
for over a fortnight. All kinds of vehicles, from
military wagons, family chariots, and mourning-
coaches at one extreme, to sedan-chairs and donkey-
carts at the other, were pressed into service. Invalids
and even those *in articulo mortis* were herded up to
the poll.

" No such scene," said a Yorkshire paper, " had been
witnessed in these islands for a hundred years as the
greatest county in them presented for fifteen days
and nights. Repose and rest have been unknown,
unless exemplified by postboys asleep in the saddle.
Every day and every night the roads leading to York
have been covered by vehicles of all kinds loaded with
voters—barouches, curricles, gigs, coaches, landaus,
dog-carts, flying wagons, mourning-coaches, and
military cars with eight horses, have left no chance for

the quiet traveller to pursue his humble journey in peace, or to find a chair at an inn to sit down upon."

As a result, Wilberforce kept his place, Viscount Milton was elected second, and Lascelles was rejected. The figures were :—

Wilberforce	.	.	.	11,806
Milton	.	.	.	11,177
Lascelles	.	.	.	10,988

Only some thirty-four thousand voters in the great shire !

It was said that Earl Fitzwilliam's expenses were £107,000 and his unsuccessful opponent's £102,000. Wilberforce, who in the fray only narrowly kept at the head of the poll, was at little expense, a public subscription which reached the sum of £64,455 having been made on his behalf. A great portion of it was afterwards returned by him. He afterwards wrote that had he not been defrauded of promised votes, his total would have reached 20,000. " However," said he, " it is unspeakable cause for thankfulness to come out of the battle ruined neither in health, character, or fortune." It was in this election that a voter who had plumped for Wilberforce and had come a long distance for the purpose, boasting that he had not spent anything on the journey, was asked how he managed it. " Sure enow," said he, " I cam all d'way ahint Lord Milton's carriage."

A story is told of a bye-election impending in Yorkshire, in which Pitt had particularly interested himself. Just upon the eve of the polling he paid a visit to the famous Mrs. B——, one of the Whig queens of the West Riding, and said, banteringly, " Well, the election is all right for us. Ten thousand guineas for the use of our side go down to Yorkshire to-night by a sure hand."

" The devil they do ! " responded Mrs. B——; and that night the bearer of the precious burden was stopped by a highwayman on the Great North Road,

and the ten thousand guineas procured the return of
the Whig candidate. The success of that robbery
was probably owing to the " sure hand " travelling
alone. Had he gone by mail-coach, the party funds
would have been safe, if we may rely upon the
bona fides of the York Post Office notice, dated
October 30, 1786, which was issued for the reassurance
of those intending to travel by mail, and says :
" Ladies and gentlemen may depend on every care and
attention being paid to their safety. They will be
guarded all the way by His Majesty's servants, and on
dark nights a postillion will ride on one of the leaders."
The notice concluded by saying that the guard was
well armed. This was no excess of caution, or merely
issued to still the nerves of timid old ladies, for at this
period we find " safety " coaches advertised, " lined
with copper, and secure against bullets " ; and recorded
encounters with armed highwaymen prove that these
precautions were not unnecessary.

VIII

York Minster, although so huge and imposing a pile
when reached, is not glimpsed by the traveller
approaching the city from the Selby route until well
within the streets, and only when Knavesmire is
passed on the Tadcaster route are its three towers
seen rising far behind the time-worn turrets of
Micklegate Bar. In bulk, it is in the very front
rank among English cathedrals, but the flatness of
its site and the narrow streets that lead to the Minster
Yard render it quite inconspicuous from any distance,
except from a few selected points and from the
commanding eyrie of the City Walls, whence, indeed,
it is seen at its grandest. " Minster " it has been
named from time immemorial, but for no apparent
reason, for York's Chapter was one of secular priests,
and as the term " minster " derives from " monas-

YORK MINSTER, FROM THE FOSS.

After   M. W. Turner, R.A.

terium," this is clearly a misnomer. But as the larger churches were those in connection with monastic rule, it must have seemed in the popular view that this gigantic church was rightly a Minster, no matter what its government.

It lies quite away from the tortuous streets by which the traveller proceeds through York for the road to the North, and it is only when nearly leaving the city by Bootham Bar that glimpses of its grey bulk are seen, at the end of some narrow lane like Stonegate or Petergate, framed in by old gabled houses that lean upon each other in every attitude suggesting age and decay, or seem to nod owlishly to neighbours just as decrepit across the cobble-stoned path. These be ideal surroundings. In the ancient shops, too, are things of rarity and price, artfully displayed to the gaze of unwary purchasers who do not know the secrets of the trade in antiques and curiosities, and are quite ignorant of the fact that they pay twice or thrice the value at such places as these for the old china, the silver, the chairs, and bookcases of quaint design that take their fancy. Only a narrow space prevents the stranger from butting up against the Minster, at the end of these lanes, for here at York we find no such wide and grassy Cathedral close as that of Winchester, or those of Canterbury, Wells, or Peterborough. Just a paved yard, extremely narrow along the whole south side and to the east, with a broader paved space at the west front, and some mingled lawns and pavements to the north, where dwell the Dean, the prebendaries, and suchlike : these are the surroundings of the Minster, which render it almost impossible to gain a comprehensive view of any part save the west front.

The Minster—the Cathedral Church of St. Peter, to call it by its proper title—is the fifth building on this site. First of all in the series was the wooden chapel erected for the baptism of Edwin, the Saxon king, in A.D. 627, followed by a stone church, begun by him in 628 and completed eight years later by King Oswald, who placed the head of Edwin, slain in battle by the heathen at Hatfield near Doncaster, here in the chapel of St. Gregory. Thirty-five years later this second church was found by Wilfrid the Archbishop to be in a state of decay, and he accordingly repaired the roofs and the walls, which he rendered " whiter than snow by means of white lime," as we are told by contemporary chroniclers. In point of fact, he whitewashed the cathedral, just as the churchwardens of a hundred years ago used to treat our village churches, for which conduct we have been reviling them for many years past, not knowing that as whitewashers they could claim such distinguished kinship. About the year 741 this second building was destroyed by fire and was replaced by another, completed in 780, itself burnt in 1069. The fourth was then begun by Thomas of Bayeux, the first Norman archbishop, and completed about 1080 ; to be in its turn partly demolished by Roger Pont l'Évêque, who about 1170 rebuilt the choir on a larger scale. Following him came Archbishop Gray, who rebuilt the south transept in its present form between 1230 and 1241 ; the north transept and the central tower in its original form being the work of John Romanus, sub-dean and treasurer from 1228 to 1256. To the son of the sub-dean, Archbishop Romanus, fell the beginning of a new nave, which was commenced by him in 1291, but was not completed until 1345, and is the existing one. All these rebuildings were on a progressive scale of size and magnificence, and so by the time they had been completed it happened that Archbishop Roger's Late Norman choir, which had replaced the smaller Early Norman one by Thomas of Bayeux, was itself regarded as too small and mean, and so was pulled down to make room for the existing choir, completed about 1400. Thus the earliest architectural features of the existing Minster above ground are the Early English transepts, and nothing remains of those vanished early buildings save some dubious Saxon masonry and Norman walling in the crypt.

The first impression gained of the exterior of York Minster—an impression which becomes only slightly modified on further acquaintance—is that of a vast, rambling, illogical mass of overdone ornament very much out of repair and very disappointing to the high expectations formed. Nor is the great central tower greatly calculated to arouse enthusiasm among those who know that of Lincoln. An immense mass, whose comparative scale is best seen from a distance, its severity of outline borders closely upon clumsiness, a defect which is heightened by its obviously unfinished condition and the clearly makeshift battlements that outrage the skyline with an effect as of an armoured champion wearing feminine headgear. It seems clear that the intention, either of the original architect of the tower, in the Early English period, or of those who re-cased it, some two hundred years later, was to carry it up another storey. The two western towers belong to much the same period, the years from 1433 to 1474, and have more than the usual commonplace appearance of the Perpendicular style. They form part of the most completely logical west front in England and almost the least inspired, excepting always that early Perpendicular fiasco, the west front of Winchester Cathedral. But the redeeming feature of York's west front is the beautiful window which, whether regarded from without or within, is one of the finest details of the building, its tracery of the flowing Decorated period narrowly approaching to the French Flamboyant style and resembling in its delicacy and complicated parts the weblike design seen on the skeleton of a leaf.

A great portion of the Minster is in the Decorated style ; not, however, conceived in the inspired vein of the west window. The nave and chapter-house cover the period of the sixty years during which Decorated Gothic flourished, and making the round of the exterior we find its characteristic mouldings and traceries repeated in a long range of seven bays, interrupted by the beautiful compositions of north and south transepts, entirely dissimilar from one

another, but individually perfect, and the most
entirely satisfactory features of the exterior. The
architects of that period were more fully endowed
with the artistic sense than those who went before,
or those who succeeded them, and their works, and
the more daring and ambitious, but something braggart,
designs of their successors, remain to prove the
contention. Eastward, beyond the transepts, extends
the long, nine-bayed choir, the view of it obscured
from the north by the protruding octagonal chapter-
house, but well seen on the south, where the soaring
ambition of its designers may advantageously be
compared with the more modest but better ordered art
of the unknown architect who built the south transept.
The architects of the choir would seem to have dared
their utmost to produce the largest windows with the
smallest proportion of wall-space, and to have at the
same time been emulative of height. With these
obvious ambitions, they have succeeded to wonderment
in rearing a building that is nearly all windows, with an
apparently dangerously small proportion of walling to
hold them together, but a building which has already
survived the storms of five hundred years structurally
and essentially sturdy and unimpaired. A great
engineering feat for that time, rather than a masterpiece
of artistry, as those who stand by and compare south
transept and choir, visible in one glance, can see.
That the perceptions of those who built the choir
were blunted is proved by the almost flat roof their
ambition for lofty walling has necessitated. With
their side walls carried up to such a height, abutting
against the central tower, they could not obtain the
steep pitch of roof which is seen on the transepts,
for a higher pitch would have committed the architectural solecism of cutting above the sills of the
great tower windows, into the windows themselves.
Thus their lofty choir is robbed of half its effect and
looks square-shouldered and ungraceful by comparison.

An odd and entirely inexplicable device is found
outside the four eastern windows of the choir clerestory,

north and south, in the placing of the triforium passage outside the building, and the screening of it and the windows with a great skeleton framework of stone. The reason of this—whether it was a mistaken idea of decoration, or for some structural strengthening purpose—is still to be sought.   But the east end is an equally crude and artless piece of work, almost wholly given up to the east window; the small flanking windows looking mean and pinched by comparison, and the abundant decoration characterised by stupid repetition and want of invention.   Here we see the Perpendicular style at a very low ebb, and thus it is not altogether a disadvantage that the road is so narrow at this point that a full view of the east end is difficult to obtain.

Criticism is at once disarmed on entering.   One enters, not by the great portals in the west front, but by the south porch, the most impressive entrance, as it happens.   For this is at once the noblest and the earliest portion of the great church, and here, in one magnificent view from south to north we obtain one of the finest architectural vistas in England.   Majesty personified, these Early English transepts are in themselves broad and long and lofty enough to furnish a nave for many another cathedral.   Spaciousness and nobility of proportion are the notes of them, and even the beautiful nave, with its aisles, light and graceful, loftier and broader than almost any other in the land, dwindles by comparison.   They produce in the surprised traveller who first beholds them the rare sensation of satisfaction, of expectations more than realised, and give an uplifting of spirit as thrilling as that caused by some inspiring passage of minstrelsy.   To stand at the crossing and gaze upwards into that vast tower which looks so clumsy to the outward view, is to receive an impression of beauty, of combined strength and lightness, which is not to be acquired elsewhere, for it is the finest of lantern towers, and, open to the vaulting of its roof, a hundred and eighty feet above the pavement, its great windows on all sides entrap the

sunbeams and shed a diffused glory on arcade and pier.
Perhaps one of the most daring attempts at effect is
that which confronts the visitor as he enters by the
south porch. Daring, not from the constructional, but
from the decorative point of view, the five equal-sized
lancet windows, the " Five Sisters " that occupy three
parts of the space in the wall of the north transept,
might so easily have been as glaring a failure as they
are a conspicuous success. Their very prominence has
doubtless given them their name, and caused the legend
to be invented of their having been the gift of five
maiden sisters. The beauty of the original Early
English glass which still remains in these lancets
has a considerable share in producing this successful
effect. That the unearthly beauty of that pale green
glass is preserved to us, together with much more in the
Minster, is due to Sir Thomas Fairfax, theParliamentary
general, himself a Yorkshireman, who kept the pious
but narrow-minded and mischievous soldiery in order,
who otherwise would have delighted in flinging prayer-
books and missals through every window in this
House of God, and have accounted it an act of religious
fervour.

We cannot explore the Minster in greater detail, for
the road yet lies in many a league before us ; nor
recount how York, city and shire, broke into rebellion
when the old religion was suppressed by Henry the
Eighth, and the Minster's treasures, particularly the
head of St. William, stolen. The Pilgrimage of Grace
was the result, in which the Yorkshire gentlemen and
others assembled, with Robert Aske at their head, and
taking as their badge the Five Wounds of Christ,
prepared to do battle for their Faith. Aske ended
on a gallows from the height of Micklegate Bar. The
same troubles recurred in the time of Elizabeth, and
Yorkshire, the last resort of Roman Catholicism, was
again in arms, with the Earls of Northumberland and
Westmoreland conspiring with the Duke of Norfolk to
release the captive Queen of Scots and restore the old
religion. The movement failed, and Northumberland

was executed on the Pavement, others being put to
death or deprived of their estates. That was the last
popular movement in favour of the old faith, and
although the city had been prelatical and Royalist
during the first years of Charles the First's reign, public

ALL SAINTS' PAVEMENT.

opinion at last veered completely round, so that
shortly after the Parliamentary victory of Marston
Moor in 1644, and the consequent surrender of the
Royalist garrison of York, the city became as Puritan
and republican as it had been the opposite. Gifts
made by Charles to the Minster were torn down and
dispersed, the very font was thrown out, and dean and
chapter were replaced by four divines elected by an
assembly. Many of the York parish churches were
wrecked by fanatics carrying out an order to destroy
" superstitious pictures and images," and nearly all
were without incumbents. When the restoration of the
monarchy and the church was effected together in 1661,

York became " one of the most factious and malignant towns in the kingdom," and two years later broke into a revolt for which twenty-one rebels were executed. The final outburst occurred in 1688, when James the Second was suspected of an intention to appoint the Roman Catholic Bishop of Callipolis to the vacant see of York. The bishop was taking part in a religious procession through the streets when an infuriated mob set upon him and seized his silver-gilt crozier, which was taken as a trophy to the vestry, where it may yet be seen. The bishop fled. A few days later James the Second ceased to reign, and with that event ended these religious contentions.

IX

BUT the stirring history of the Minster itself was not yet completed, for the final chapter in a long record of events was not enacted until the early years of the nineteenth century.

The roads in the neighbourhood of York on February 2, 1829, were thronged with excited crowds hurrying to the city. Dashing through them came the fire-engines of Leeds, and others from Escrick Park. Far ahead, a great column of smoke hovered in the cold February sky. York Minster was on fire.

It was no accident that had caused this conflagration, but the wild imaginings of one Jonathan Martin, which had prompted him to become the incendiary of that stately pile. A singular character, compacted of the unlovely characteristics of Mawworm and the demented prophet, Solomon Eagle, this was the crowning act of a life distinguished by religious mania. Jonathan Martin was born at Hexham in 1782, and apprenticed to a tanner. His parents were poor, and he had only the slightest kind of education. At the expiration of his apprenticeship he found himself in London, and was speedily entrapped by the press-gang and sent to serve his Majesty as an able seaman. It seems to have been at this period that the unbalanced state of his mind first became noticeable. He was with the fleet at many places, and often in action, from Copenhagen to the Nile. At times he would exhibit cowardice, and at others either indifference to danger or actual bravery. He would be religious, dissolute, industrious, idle, sulky, or cheerful by turns : a pretended dreamer of dreams and communicant with angels. " Parson Saxe," his shipmates named him ; " but," said one, years afterwards, " I always thought him more rogue than fool."

Martin was paid off in 1810. He settled to work for a farmer at Norton, near Durham, and shortly afterwards married. He became a member of the Wesleyan Methodist body at Norton, and began those religious exercises which he claims to have converted him and to have emancipated him from the law, being " justified by faith " only. How dangerous such views of personal irresponsibility can be when held by the weak-minded his after-career was only too plainly to show. He immediately conceived an abhorrence of the Church of England, as a church teaching obedience to pastors and masters, and of the clergy for their worldliness. In this last respect, indeed, Martin—as we think now—had no little justification, for the Church had not then begun to arise from the almost Pagan slough of laziness, indifference, and greed of wealth and good living which throughout the previous century had marked the members of the Establishment, from the country parson up to the archbishops. When clergymen could find it in them to perform the solemn rite of the burial service while in a state of drunkenness ; when, under Martin's own observation at Durham, the Prince-Bishop of that city enjoyed emoluments and perquisites amounting to £30,000 per annum, there is little cause for surprise that hatred and contempt of the cloth should arise.

This basis of justification, acting upon a mind already diseased, and not rendered more healthy by fasting and brooding over the Scriptures, resulted in his attempting to preach from church pulpits, in writing threatening letters to the clergy, and eventually to a silly threat to shoot the Bishop of Oxford when at Stockport. For this he was rightly confined in a lunatic asylum at Gateshead. Some months later he managed to escape, and after wandering about the country took service with his former employer at Norton, the magistrates consenting to his remaining at liberty. In 1822 he left for Darlington, where he lived until 1827. His wife had died while he was in the asylum, and in 1828, while engaged in hawking a pamphlet biography of himself at Boston, he made the acquaintance of a young woman of that town and married her. By this time his religious mania had grown worse, and when, on December 26, 1828, he and his wife journeyed to York, it would appear that he went there with the design of burning the Cathedral already half-formed. He haunted the building day by day, leaving denunciatory letters from time to time. One, discovered on the iron grille of the choir screen, exhorted the clergy to " repent and cry For marcey for know is the day of vangens and your Cumplet Destruction is at Hand for the Lord will not sufer you and the Deveal and your blind Hellish Docktren to dseve the works of His Hands no longer. . . . Depart you Carsit blind Gides in to the Hotest plase of Hell to be tormentid with the Deveal and all his Eanguls for Ever and Ever."

Violent language ! but one may hear harangues very like it any day within Hyde Park, by the Marble Arch. There are many incendiaries in the making around us to-day, and as little attention is paid to them as to Martin's ravings.

Undoubtedly mad, he possessed something of the madman's cunning, and with the plan of firing the Cathedral fully formed, set out with his wife for Leeds, as he gave out, on the 27th of January. At Leeds he remained a few days, and was remarkable for his unusually quiet and orderly behaviour. He left on Saturday morning, ostensibly for Tadcaster, saying he should return on the Monday ; but went instead to

JONATHAN MARTIN, INCENDIARY.

Drawn in gaol at York Castle by the Rev. J. Kilby.

York. Here the madman's cunning broke down, for he
stayed at a place where he was well known; at the
lodgings, in fact, that he had left a few days before.
He prowled about the Cathedral the whole of the next
day, Sunday, and attended service there, hiding
behind a tomb in the north transept; overheard the
notes of the organ—the finest in England—thundering
and booming and rolling in echoes amid the fretted
roofs. The sound troubled the brain of the maniac.
" Buzz, buzz," he whispered; " I'll teach thee to stop
thy buzzing," and hid, shivering with religious and
lunatic ecstasy, in the recess until the building was
empty.

The short February day closed, and left the Cathedral
in darkness; but he still waited. The ringers paid
their evening-visit to the belfry, and he watched them
from his hiding-place. He watched them go and then
began his work. The ringers had left the belfry
unlocked. Ascending to it, he cut a length of about
a hundred feet off the prayer-bell rope, and, with his
sailor's handiness, made a rough ladder of it, by which
to escape. Those were the days before lucifer matches.
He had come provided with a razor, which he used as a
steel; a flint, tinder, and a penny candle cut in two.
Climbing, then, into the choir, he made two piles on the
floor of prayer-books, curtains, hassocks, and cushions,
and taking a candle from the altar, cut it up and
distributed it between the two. Then, setting light to
them, he set to work to escape. He had taken a pair
of pincers from the shoemaker with whom he lodged,
and breaking with them a window in the north transept,
he hauled his rope through, and descended into the
Minster Yard, soon after three o'clock in the morning.

The fire was not discovered until four hours later.
By that time the stalls were half-consumed, and the
vestry, where the communion plate was kept, was on
fire. The plate was melted into an unrecognisable
mass. By eight o'clock, despite the exertions of many
willing helpers, the organ-screen was burnt, and the
organ-pipes fell in thunder to the pavement, to the

accompaniment of a furious shower of molten lead from the roof, which was now burning.   The city fire-engines, those of the Cathedral, and others from Leeds and Escrick were all playing upon the conflagration that day, and the 7th Dragoon Guards and the Militia helped with a will, or kept back the vast crowds which had poured into the city from far and near.   It was not until evening that the fire was quenched, and by that time the roof of the choir, over 130 feet in length, had been destroyed, and with it the stalls, the Bishop's throne, and all the mediæval enrichments of that part of the building.   Curiously   enough,   the   great   east window was but little damaged.   The cost of this madman's   act   was   put   at   £100,000.   A   singular coincidence, greatly remarked upon at the time, was that on the Sunday following this disaster, one of the lessons for the day was the sixty-fourth chapter of Isaiah, the Church's prayer to God, of which one verse at least was particularly applicable : " Our holy and our beautiful house, where our fathers praised Thee, is burned with fire ; and all our pleasant things are laid waste."

Martin was, in the first instance, connected with the outrage by the evidence of the shoemaker's pincers he had left behind him.   They were identified by his landlord.   Meanwhile, the incendiary had fled along the Great North Road ; first to Easingwold, thirteen miles away, where he drank a pint of ale ; and then tramping on to Thirsk.   Thence he hurried to North-allerton, arriving at three o'clock in the afternoon, worn out with thirty-three miles of walking.   That night he journeyed in a coal-cart to West Auckland, and so eventually to a friend near Hexham, in whose house he was arrested on the 6th of February.   Taken to York, he was tried at the sessions at York Castle on March 30th.   The verdict, given on the following day, was " not guilty, on the ground of insanity," and he was ordered to be kept in close custody during his Majesty's pleasure.   Martin was shortly afterwards removed from York Castle to St. Luke's Hospital,

YORK MINSTER ON FIRE, ON THE NIGHT OF MAY 20th, 1840.

From a Con emporary Prin

E

London, in which he died in 1838. Two years later, the Minster was again on fire, this time as the result of an accident, and the western tower was burnt out.

Insanity in some degree ran through the Martin family. His brother John, who died in 1854, was a prominent artist, whose unbalanced mind did not give way, but led him to paint extraordinary pictures, chiefly of Scriptural interest and apocalyptic horrors. He was in his day considered a genius, and many of his terrific imaginations were engraved and must yet be familiar : such pictures as " Belshazzar's Feast," " The Eve of the Deluge," " The Last Man," and " The Plains of Heaven " : pictures well calculated to give children nightmares.

X

WE must now leave York for the North. To do so, we proceed through Bootham Bar, where the taxis linger that ply between the city and the railway station.

Let us glance back upon the picturesque sky-line of City and Minster and read, maybe, the modern explanatory historical inscription placed on the ancient Bar. Thus :—

" Entry from North through Forest of Galtres. In old times armed men were stationed here to watch, and to conduct travellers through the forest and protect them against the wolves.

" The Royal Arms were taken down in 1650, when Cromwell passed through, against Scotland. Heads of three rebels exposed here, for attempting to restore Commonwealth, 1663.

" Erected on Roman foundation, probably early in 13th centy.

" Interior rebuilt with freestone, 1719.

" The portcullis remains."

So, in those ancient times when the Forest of Galtres lay immediately before you on passing out of Bootham

Bar and going North—the forest with wolves and bandits—you stepped not into a suburb, but came directly off the threshold into the wild.

To-day, outside the walls we come at once into the district of Clifton, after Knavesmire the finest suburb of

BOOTHAM BAR.

York; the wide road lined with old mansions that almost reek of prebendal appointments, J.P.'s, incomes of over two thousand a year, and butlers. It is true that there are those which cannot be included in this category, but they are here on sufferance and as a foil to the majesty of their superiors, just as the Lunatic Asylum a little farther down the road gives, or should give, by contrast a finer flavour to the lives of those who have not to live in it. There is another pleasing thing at Clifton, in the altogether charming new building of the " White Horse " inn, which seems to hint that they have at last begun to recover the lost art in Yorkshire of

building houses that are not vulgar or hideous. It is
full time.

Would you see a charming village church, a jewel in
its sort ? Then, when reaching Skelton, three miles
onward, explore the bye-road at the back of the
village, over whose clustered few roofs its Early English
bell-cote peeps. But a moment, please, before we
reach it. This " bye-road " is the original highway.
and the " back " of the village street its old front,
There is a moral application somewhere in these altered
circumstances for those who have the wit, the
inclination, and the opportunity to seek it.

The improved road, a hundred years old, is carried
straight and level past the rear of the cottages, and the
rugged old one goes serpentining past the front doors,
where the entrance to the " Bay Horse " looks out

SKELTON CHURCH.

across a little green to where the church stands, the
faded old Bay Horse himself wondering where the
traffic that use to pass this way has all gone to. The
signs of the " Bay Horse " and the " Yorkshire Grey "
are, by the way, astonishingly frequent on the Great
North Road.

But the church. It is an unpretending building, without a tower, and only a bell-cote rising from its broad roof; but perfect within its limits. Early English throughout, with delicately-cut mouldings, beautiful triple lancets at the east end, and fine porch, the green and grey harmonies of its slate roof and well-preserved stonework, complete a rarely satisfying picture. A legend, still current, says it was built from stone remaining over after the building of the south transept of York Cathedral, in 1227. The Church in the Wood it was then, for from the gates of York to Easingwold, a distance of thirteen miles, stretched that great Forest of Galtres, through which, to guide wandering travellers, as we have already seen, the lantern-tower and burning cresset of All Saints in the Pavement, at York, were raised aloft.

Red deer roamed the Forest of Galtres, and bandits not so chivalrous as Robin Hood; so few dared to explore its recesses unarmed and unaccompanied. But where in olden times these romantic attendants of, or dissuading circumstances from travel existed, we have now only occasional trees and an infinity of flat roads, past Shipton village to Tollerton Cross Lanes and Easingwold. This country is dulness personified. The main road is flat and featureless, and the branch roads instinct with a melancholy emptiness that hives in every ditch and commonplace hedgerow. A deadly sameness, a paralysing negation, closes the horizon of this sparsely settled district, depopulated in that visitation of fire and sword when William the Conqueror came, in 1069, and massacred a hundred thousand of those who had dared to withstand him. They had surrendered on promise of their lives and property being respected, but the fierce Norman utterly destroyed the city of York and laid waste the whole of the country between York and Durham. Those who were not slain perished miserably of cold and famine. Their pale ghosts still haunt the route of the Great North Road and afflict it, though more than eight hundred years have flown.

Now comes Easingwold ; grimly bare and gritty wide street, with narrow pavements and broad selvedges of cobbles sloping from them down into a roadway filled, not with traffic, but with children at noisy play. Shabby houses lining this street, houses little better than cottages, and ugly at that ; grey, hard-featured, forbidding. Imagine half a mile of this, with a large church on a knoll away at the northern end, and you have Easingwold. One house is interesting. It is easily identified, because it is the only one of any architectural character in the place. Now a school, it was once the chief coaching and posting establishment, under the sign of the " Rose and Crown," and in those times kept five post boys, and, by consequence, twenty horses, others being kept for the " Wellington " and " Express" coaches which Lacy, the landlord, used to horse on the Easingwold to Thirsk stage. The " New Inn," although an inferior house, was the place at which the Royal mail and the " Highflyer " changed.

An old post boy of the " Rose and Crown " survived until recent years, in the person of Tommy Hutchinson. Originally a tailor, he early forsook the board and the needle for the pigskin and the whip. If a tailor be the ninth part of a man, certainly the weazened postboys (who ever saw a fat one ?) of old were themselves only fractions, so far as appearance went ; and accordingly Tommy was not badly suited. But a power of endurance was contained within that spare frame, and he eclipsed John Blagg of Retford's hundred and ten miles' day on one occasion, riding post five times from Easingwold to York and back, a distance of a hundred and thirty miles. Tommy used to express an utter contempt for " bilers on wheels," as he called loco-motives. " Ah divvent see nowt in 'em," he would say ; " ye can't beat a po'shay and good horses." Peace be with him !

That rare thing on the Great North Road, a rise, leads out of Easingwold, past unkempt cottages, to "White House Inn," a mile and a half distant, where the inn buildings, now farmhouses, but still brilliantly whitewashed, stand on either side of the road, in a lonely spot near where the Kyle stream, like a flowing ditch, oozes beneath Dawnay Bridge.

The " White House " was the scene of a murder in 1623. At that time the innkeeper was a certain Ralph Raynard, who " kept company " with a girl in service at Red House, Thornton Bridge. The lovers quarrelled, and in a pique the girl married a farmer named Fletcher, of Moor House, Raskelfe. Unhappily, she did not love the man she had married, while she certainly did retain an affection for her old sweetheart, and he for her. Going between Raskelfe and Easing-wold on market-days on her horse, she would often stop at the " White House," and chat with Ralph Raynard; the ostler, Mark Dunn, minding the horse when she dismounted. Raynard's sister kept house with him at the inn, and she saw that no good could come of these visits, but he would not listen to her warnings, and the visits continued. It was not long before Fletcher's neighbours began to hint to him something of these little flirtations of his wife with her old lover; and one evening he caught the ostler of the " White House" in his orchard, where he was waiting for an opportunity to deliver a message from Raynard to her. The man returned to the inn without having fulfilled his mission, and smarting from a thrashing he had received at the hands of the indignant farmer. Shortly after this, Fletcher had occasion to go a journey. Things had not been going well with him latterly, and his home was rendered unhappy by the evidence of his wife's dislike of him. Little wonder then, that he had dismal forebodings as he set out. Before leaving, he wrote on a sheet of paper :—

If I should be missing, or suddenly wanted be,
Mark Ralph Raynard, Mark Dunn, and mark my wife for me,

addressing it to his sister.

No sooner was he gone than Mrs. Fletcher mounted her horse and rode to Raskelfe, where, with Raynard and Mark Dunn, a murderous plot was contrived for

putting Fletcher out of the way. They were waiting
for him when he returned at evening, and as he stood
a moment on Dawnay Bridge, where the little river
runs beneath the highway, two of them rushed upon
him and threw him into the water. It would be
difficult for a man to drown here, but the innkeeper
and the ostler leapt in after him, and as he lay there
held his head under water, while his wife seized his feet.
When the unfortunate man was quite dead they thrust
his body into a sack, and, carrying their burden with
them to the inn, buried it in the garden, Raynard
sowing some mustard-seed over the spot. This took
place on the 1st of May. On the 7th of July, Raynard
went to Topcliffe Fair, and put up at the " Angel."
Going into the stable, he was confronted by the
apparition of the unhappy Fletcher, glowing with a
strange light and predicting retribution. He rushed
out among the booths, and tried to think he had been
mistaken. Coming to a booth where they sold small
trinkets, he thought he would buy a present for his
sweetheart, and, taking up a chain of coral beads,
asked the stallkeeper how it looked on the neck.
To his dismay the apparition stood opposite, with a red
chain round *its* neck, with its head hanging to one side,
like that of an executed criminal, while a voice informed
him that presently he and his accomplices should be
wearing hempen necklaces.

When night had fallen he mounted his horse and rode
for home. On the way, at a spot called the Carr, he
saw something in the road. It was a figure emerging
from a sack and shaking the water off it, like a
Newfoundland dog. With a yell of terror the haunted
man dug his heels into his horse and galloped madly
away ; but the figure, irradiated by a phosphorescent
glimmer and dragging an equally luminous sack after it,
was gliding in front of him all the while, at an equal
pace, and so continued until the " White House " was
reached, where it slid through the garden hedge and
into the ground where Fletcher's body had been laid.

Raynard's sister was waiting for him, with supper

ready, and with a dish of freshly-cut mustard. *She* did not see the spectre sitting opposite, pointing a minatory finger at that dreadful salad, but *he* did, and terrified, confessed to the crime. Sisterly affection was not proof against this, and she laid information against the three accomplices before a neighbouring Justice of the Peace, Sir William Sheffield of Raskelfe Park. They were committed to York Castle, tried, and hanged on July 28, 1623. The bodies were afterwards cut down and taken to the inn, being gibbeted near the scene of the crime, on a spot still called Gallows Hill, where the bones of the three malefactors were accidentally ploughed up over a hundred and twenty years ago.

If its surroundings may be said to fit in with a crime, then this seems an ideal spot for the commission of dark deeds, this eerie place where an oozy plantation, or little wood, is placed beside the road, its trees standing in pools or on moss-grown tussocks ; the road in either direction a solitude.

Raskelfe, or " Rascall," as it is generally called, lies away from the road. It has a church which still possesses a wooden tower, and the local rhyme,

> Wooden church, wooden steeple,
> Rascally church, and rascally people.

is yet heard in the mouths of depreciatory neighbours.

XI

The Hambleton Hills now come in sight, and close in the view on the right hand, at a distance of five miles ; running parallel with the road as far as North-allerton ; sullen hills, with the outlines of mountains, and wanting only altitude to earn the appellation. The road, in sympathy with its nearness to them, goes up and down in jerky rises and falls, passing the outlying houses of Thormanby and the farmsteads of Birdforth, which pretends, with its mean little church,

like a sanctified cow-shed, to be a village—and signally
fails.

The gates of Thirkleby Park and the " Griffin " inn,
standing where a toll-gate formerly stood on what was
once Bagby Common, bring one past a bye-road which
leads to Coxwold, five miles away, and to the Hambleton
White Horse, a quite unhistorical imitation, cut in the
hillside in 1857, of its prehistoric forerunners in
Berkshire and Wilts. Coxwold is a rarely pretty
village, famous as having been the living of the
Reverend Laurence Sterne from 1760 to 1768. The
house he lived in, now divided into three cottages, is
the place where *Tristram Shandy* was finished and the
Sentimental Journey written. " Shandy Hall " it is
called, " shandy " being the local dialect-word for
" crazy."

Thirsk lies less than three miles ahead. There have
been those who have called it " picturesque." Let us
pity them, for those to whom Thirsk shows a picturesque
side must needs have acquaintance with only the
sorriest and most commonplace of towns. The place is,
in fact, a larger Easingwold, with the addition of a
market-place like that of Selby—after the abbey has
been subtracted from it ! There are Old Thirsk and
New Thirsk, the new town called into existence by the
railway, a mile to the west. The " Three Tuns,"
" Crown," and " Fleece " were the three coaching inns
of Thirsk, and still show their hard-featured faces to the
grey, gaunt streets. The one pretty " bit " is encountered after having left the town behind. Passing the
church, the road is bordered by the beautiful broad
sheet of water formed by damming the Caldbeck.
Looking backwards, the view is charming, with the
church-tower coming into the composition, a glance to
the left including the Hambleton Hills.

The hamlet of Thornton-le-Street, which derives its
name from standing on an old Roman road, is a tiny
place with a small church full of large monuments,
and the remains of a huge old posting establishment,
once familiar to travellers as the " Spotted Dog,"

standing on either side of the road.   One side appears
to be empty, and the other is now the post office.
A graceful clump of poplars now shades the sharp bend

THE "SPOTTED DOG," THORNTON-LE-STREET.

where the road descends, past the lodge-gates of the
Hall, the seat of the Earl of Cathcart.   Presently the
road climbs again to the crest whence Thornton-le-Moor
may be glimpsed on the left, and thence goes, leaving
the singularly named Thornton-le-Beans on the right,
in commonplace fashion to Northallerton.

As are Easingwold and Thirsk, so is Northallerton.
Let that suffice for its aspect, and let us to something
of its story, which practically begins in 1138, at the
battle of Northallerton, dimly read of in schooldays,
and still capable of conferring an interest upon the

locality, even though the site of that old-time struggle on Standard Hill is three miles away to the north on Cowton Moor. The position of the townlet, directly in the line of march of Scots descending to harry the English, and of the English marching to punish those hairy-legged Caledonians, led to many plunderings and burnings, and to various scenes of retribution, enacted in the streets or along the road ; and although Northallerton must nowadays confess to a mile-long dulness, time cannot have hung heavily with its inhabitants when the Scots burnt their houses in 1319 and again in 1322 ; when the rebel Earls of 1569 were executed near the church ; when the Scottish army held Charles the First prisoner here in 1647, or when— last scene in its story—the Duke of Cumberland encamped on the hillsides in 1745.

The name of Allerton is said to derive from the Anglo-Saxon *aelr*, an alder tree, and many are the Allertons of sorts in Yorkshire. Its central feature— which, however, is not geographically central, but at the northern end of the one long street—is the church, large and with a certain air of nobility which befits the parish church of such a place as Northallerton, anciently the capital of a " soke," and still giving a name to the " Northallertonshire " district of Yorkshire. The old coaching inns of the town, like those of so many other northern towns and villages on this road, are not impressive to the Southerner, who, the further north he progresses, is, with Dr. Johnson, still more firmly convinced that he is leaving the finest fruits of civilisation behind him. First now, as then, is the " Golden Lion," large but not lovely ; the inn referred to as the " Black Swan " by Sydney Smith when writing to Lady Grey, advising her how to journey from London, in the passage, " Do not set off too soon, or you will be laid up at the ' Black Swan,' Northallerton, or the ' Elephant and Castle,' Borough-bridge ; and your bill will come to a thousand pounds, besides the waiter." The true sportsman who reads these lines will put up at the " Golden Lion " to test whether or not the reverend humorist is out of date as regards the tariff ; nor will he forget to try the North-allerton ale, to determine if Master George Meryon's verse, written in the days of James the Second, is still topical :—

Northallerton, in Yorkshire, doth excell
All England, nay, all Europe, for strong yell.

The " Golden Lion " was, at the close of the coaching era, the foremost inn at Northallerton, and at its doors the " Wellington " London and Newcastle coach changed teams until the railway ran it off the road. The Edinburgh mail changed at the " Black Bull," which survives as an inn, but only half its original size, the other half now being a draper's shop. The " King's Head," another coaching-house, has quite retired into private life, while the " Old Golden Lion," not a very noted coaching establishment, except, perhaps, for the bye-roads, remains much the same as ever.

XII

AT Northallerton we reach the junction of the alternative route, which, branching from the Selby and York itinerary, goes over difficult, but much more beautiful, country by way of Wetherby and Boroughbridge. The ways diverge at the northern extremity of Doncaster, and as both can equally claim to be an integral part of the Great North Road, it is necessary to go back these sixty-three miles to that town and explore the route. Beginning at a left-hand fork by the flat meadows that border the river Don, it comes in a mile to York Bar, a name recalling the existence of a turnpike-gate, whose disappearance so recently as 1879 seems to bring us strangely near old coaching days. The toll-house still stands, and with the little inn beyond, backed and surrounded by tall trees, forms a pleasant peep down the long flat road. " Red House," nearly three miles onward, is plainly indicated by its flaring red-painted walls. Now a farmhouse, it was once a small coaching-inn

YORK BAR·

principally concerned with the traffic along the Wakefield road, which branches off here to the left. Passing this, we come in two miles to Robin Hood's Well, a group of houses by Skelbrooke Park, where at the " New Inn " and the " Robin Hood " many coaches changed horses daily, the passengers taking the opportunity of drinking from Robin Hood's Well, a spring connected with that probably mythical outlaw, who is said to have met the Bishop of Hereford travelling along the road at this spot, and to have not only held him to heavy ransom, but to have compelled him to dance an undignified jig round an oak in Skelbrooke Park, on a spot still called (now the tree itself has disappeared) " Bishop's Tree Root." Among famous travellers who have sipped of the crystal spring of Robin Hood's Well is Evelyn, who journeyed this way in 1654. " Near it," he says, " is a stone chaire; and an iron ladle to drink out of, chained to the seat,"

ROBIN HOOD'S WELL.

Some fifty years later, the very ugly building that now covers the spring was erected by Vanbrugh for the Earl of Carlisle. It cannot be said to add much to the romantic associations of the place, but the efforts of the wayfarers, who in two centuries have carved every available inch of its surface with their names, render it a curious sight.

Here the road begins a long climb up to the spot where five ways meet, the broad left-hand road conducting into Leeds. This is, or was, Barnsdale Bar, where some of the local Leeds coaches branched from the Great North Road, the chief ones between London and Leeds continuing along this route as far as Peckfield Turnpike, five miles to the other side of Ferrybridge. Barnsdale Bar is, like all the other toll-bars, a thing of the past, but the old toll-house still hides among the trees by the roadside. Beyond it the way lies along an exposed road high up on the hill-tops ; a lonely stretch of country where it is a peculiarly ill mischance to be caught in a storm. Thence it plunges suddenly into the deep gorge of Went Bridge, where the little river Went goes with infantile fury among rocks and mossy boulders along a winding course thickly overhung with trees. The wooded sides of this narrow valley are picturesque in the highest degree, but were probably not highly appreciated by timid coach-passengers who, having been driven down the precipitous road at one side at the peril of their lives, were turned out by the guard to ease the toiling horses by walking up the corresponding ascent at the other. This is the prettiest spot in all " merry Barnsdale," and anciently one of those most affected by Robin Hood. His very degenerate successors, the poachers and cut-throats of James the First's time, found it a welcome harbourage and foregathered at the predecessor of the Old Blue Bell Inn, which was accordingly deprived of its license for some time. The old sign, bearing the date of 1633, when business was probably resumed, is still kept within the house, as the rhymed inscription on the modern one outside informs the passer-by :—

The Ble Bell on Wentbridge Hill,
The old sign is existing still
Inside the house.

An old posting-inn, the " Bay Horse," has long since reverted to the condition of a private house.

The road rising out of Went Bridge runs between the jagged rocks of a cutting made in the last years of the coaching age to lighten the pull up, but still it is a formidable climb. This is followed by a hollow where a few outlying houses of Darrington village are seen, and then the bleak high tableland is reached that has to be traversed before the road drops down into the valley of the Aire at Ferrybridge, that now dull and grimy town which bears no appearance of

having had an historic past.   Yet Ferrybridge was
the scene of the skirmish that heralded the battle of
Towton, and stands in the midst of that mediæval
cockpit of England, wherein for centuries so many rival
factions contended together.   Near by is Pontefract,
in whose castle Richard the Second met a mysterious
death, and not far off lies Wakefield.   Towton Field
itself lies along the Tadcaster route to York.   In every
direction blood has been shed, for White Rose or Red,
for King or Parliament ; but Ferrybridge is anything
but romantic to the eye, however greatly its associations may appeal to the well-stored mind.   Coal-mining
and quarrying industries overlie these things.   The
place-name explains the situation of the townlet
sufficiently well, and refers to the first building of a
bridge over the old-time ferry by which wayfarers
crossed the Aire to Brotherton, on the opposite bank.
It is quite unknown when the first bridge was built,
but one existed here in 1461, the year when Towton
fight was fought.   This was succeeded by a wooden
structure, itself replaced by the present substantial
stone bridge, built at the beginning of the eighteenth
century.   This was always a troublesome part of the
road to keep in repair, as we may judge from old
records.   A forty days' indulgence was granted by
the Bishop of Durham early in the fourteenth century
to the faithful who would contribute to the repair of the
road between Ferrybridge and Brotherton, in these
words :—" Persuaded that the minds of the faithful
are more ready to attach themselves to pious works
when they have received the salutary encouragement
of fuller indulgences, trusting in the mercy of God
Almighty and the merits and prayers of the glorious
Virgin his Mother, of St. Peter, St. Paul, and of the
most holy confessor Cuthbert, our patron, and of all
saints, we remit forty days of the penances imposed
on all our parishioners and others, sincerely contrite
and confessed of their sins, who shall help by their
charitable gifts, or by their bodily labour, in the
building or in the maintenance of the causeway

between Brotherton and Ferrybridge, where a great many people pass by."

Let us hope that the pious, thus incited to the commission of good works, responded. It was a more serious matter, however, in later ages, when a great many more people passed by, and when road-surveyors, unable to dispense these ghostly favours, repaired the roads only at the pecuniary expense of the ratepayers. These Yorkshire streams, the Aire, the Wharfe, and many others, descending from the high moorlands, develop an extraordinary force in times of flood, and have often destroyed half the communications of these districts. Such was the havoc wrought in 1795 that many of the bridges were washed away and great holes made in the roads. Three bridges on this road between Doncaster and Ferrybridge disappeared. With such perils threatened, travellers deserved to be comfortably housed when they lay by for the night. And comfort was the especial feature of these inns.

The most luxurious inn and posting-house in the north of England was held to be the "Swan" at Ferrybridge; "in 1737 and since the best inn upon the great northern road," according to Scott. However that may have been, certainly the "Angel" at Ferrybridge was the largest. Both, however, have long since been given up. The many scattered buildings of the "Angel" have become private houses, and the "Swan," empty for many years past, is falling into a roofless ruin by the riverside. Innkeeping was no mean trade in those times, especially when allied with the proprietorship of horses and coaches. Thus, in the flower of the coaching age, the "Angel" was in the hands of a medical man, a certain Dr. Alderson, the son of a local clergyman, who actually found time to attend properly to his practice and to conduct the business of a licensed victualler and coach-proprietor. He thought it not derogatory to his social position to be "mine host," and he certainly made many friends by his enterprise. Ferrybridge, as the branching-off place of yet another Great North Road route—the Tadcaster route to York—was a very busy coaching centre, and besides the two inns mentioned there were the " Greyhound " and the " Golden Lion." The last-named was especially the drovers' house. Drovers were a great feature of the road in these old days, and their flocks and herds an unmitigated nuisance to all other travellers. Uncouth creatures from Scotland, they footed it all the way to London with their beasts, making their twenty miles a day; their sheep and cattle often numerous enough to occupy a whole mile of road, and raising dust-clouds dense enough to choke a whole district. It was, at the pace they went, a three weeks' journey from the far north to London and the fat cattle that started on the four hundred miles walk must, with these efforts, have become the leanest of kine on arrival at Smithfield.

The " Old Fox " inn, which still stands on the other side of the river at Brotherton, was also a drovers' place of call. It stands at the actual fork of the roads, eleven miles from Tadcaster, and twenty from York. The Edinburgh mail originally ran this way, finally changing to the Selby route, while the " Highflyer " and " Wellington," London and Edinburgh and London and Newcastle, coaches kept on it until the end in 1840; but it was chiefly crowded with the cross-country coach traffic, which was a very heavy one.

The places are few and uninteresting on these twenty miles into York; Sherburn and Tadcaster—that town of ales—the chief of them; while the tiny godless village of Towton, without a church, on the way, is disappointing to the pilgrim, eager to see it for the sake of its association with the great battle. The road skirts the eastern side of that tragic field, after passing the hamlet of Barkston Ash.

XIII

THE battle of Towton, March 29, 1461, was the bloodiest ever fought on English ground, the slain on both sides in that desperate fight and in the skirmishes at Ferrybridge and Dintingdale amounting to more than 30,000 men. The events that had preceded it were alternately cheering and depressing to the hopes of the Yorkists, who had been defeated with great slaughter at Wakefield on the last day but one of the previous December, had gained the important victory of Mortimer's Cross on the 2nd of February, and had been defeated again at the second battle of St. Albans on the 17th of the same month; and although on March 4th the young Duke of York had entered London and assumed the crown as Edward the Fourth, the Lancastrians still held the Midlands and, lying at York, interposed a bold front against an advance. It was a singular position. The Lancastrians had their headquarters at the city from which their opponents took their title, and two kings of England, equally matched in power, animated their respective adherents with the utmost loyalty.

After their victory at St. Albans the Lancastrians, exhausted, had retired to York, the south being as dangerous to a Lancastrian army as the north, loyal to the Red Rose, was to the Yorkists. The Yorkists, on their part, eager to enter London, did not pursue their rivals. Both sides required breathing time, for events had marched too rapidly in the past two months for the pace to be maintained. Still, the Yorkists were in force, three weeks later, at Pontefract, and threatening to cross the Aire at Ferrybridge, a strategic point on their contemplated line of advance to the city of York. It was here, early in the morning of the 28th, that the bloody prelude to the battle opened, in a sudden Lancastrian attack on the Yorkist outpost. Lord Fitzwalter, the Yorkist commander, lay asleep in bed at the time. Seizing a pole-axe at his sudden awakening, he was slain almost instantly, but his force, succeeding in driving the enemy across the river, took up a position at Brotherton, the Lancastrians falling back in disorder to Dintingdale, near Barkston Ash, where, later in the

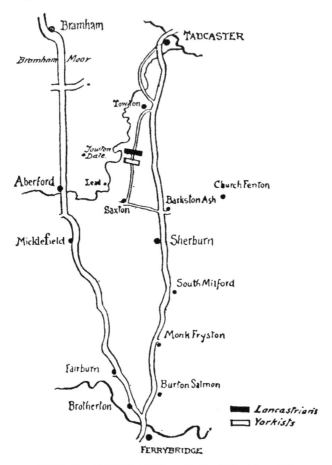

THE BATTLEFIELD OF TOWTON AND
SURROUNDING COUNTRY.

day, the Lancastrian, Lord Clifford, was slain by an arrow. The advance-guard of the Lancastrian army now fell back upon the main body, which took up a well-chosen position between the villages of Saxton and Towton, lying across a rising road which led out of the former place, and having on its right the steeply falling meadows leading down into the deep depression of

Towton Dale, where the Cock Beck still wanders in far-flung loops in the flat lands below. On their left the ground stretched away for some distance and then fell gently towards the flats of Church Fenton. At their

SAXTON.

rear the road descended steeply again into Towton, while Tadcaster lay three miles and York eleven miles beyond. It was a position of great strength and one that could only possibly be turned from the left. The fatal defect of it lay in the chance, in the case of defeat, of the beaten army being disorganised by a retreat down so steep a road, leading as it did to the crossing of a stream swollen with winter rains.

In visiting this spot, we must bear in mind that the broad road from Ferrybridge to Tadcaster and York was not then in existence. The way lay across the elevated land which, rising from Barkston Ash towards Saxton, reaches to a considerable height between that village and Towton. From this commanding spot the valleys of the Wharfe and Ouse lie plainly unfolded, and the towers of York itself may be seen on the skyline, on the verge of this wide expanse of meadows and woodlands.

The hedgerows on the way to the battle-field are remarkable for the profusion of briar roses that grow here in place of the more usual blackberry brambles and thorns, and Bloody Meadow, the spot where the thickest of the fight took place, was until quite recently thickly overgrown with the red and white roses with

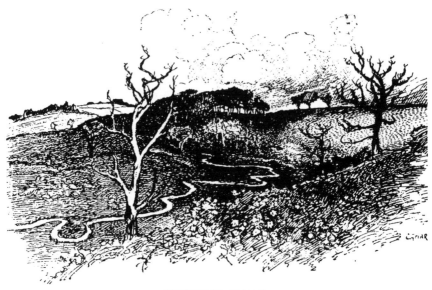

TOWTON DALE.

which Nature had from time immemorial planted this scene of strife. Latterly they have all been grubbed up by farmers, keener on the purity of their grasslands than on historic associations.

The main body of the Yorkists, advancing to Saxton, opened the attack on the Lancastrians early in the morning of Palm Sunday, the 29th. The centre of the fight was in the meadow on the left hand of the road leading towards Towton, a short distance beyond Towton Dale quarry. The Lancastrians numbered 60,000 men, the Yorkists 48,600. For ten hours the furious encounter raged, " sore fought, for hope of life was set aside on every part." Six years' warfare, from 1455, when the first battle of St. Albans had been fought, had rendered the enemies implacable. Almost every combatant had already lost kinsfolk, and intense hatred caused the order on both sides that no quarter was to be given and no prisoners taken. The day was bitterly cold, and snowstorms swept the upland, driving in the faces of the Lancastrians with such blinding fury that their arrows, shot in reply to the Yorkist volleys, could not be properly aimed, and so missed their mark. A hand-to-hand encounter with swords and battle-axes then followed, obstinately fought, but resulting practically in the butchery of the Lancastrians, for nearly the half of their whole force were slain or met their death either in Towton Dale or at the crossing of the stream down the road past Towton Hall. The rest fled to Tadcaster and on to York, where Henry the Sixth, the Queen, and the young Prince of Wales were waiting the result of the fight. They left immediately, and the victorious Duke of York entered the ancient city.

Many proud nobles fell that day with the men-at-arms; among others, Lord Dacre, fighting for the Red Rose, shot by a boy concealed in what the country people call a " bur-tree," that is to say, an elder. He lies buried in the churchyard of Saxton, on the north side of the church, under a much-mutilated altar-tomb, whose inscription refers to him as " verus miles "—a true knight. Tradition yet tells of his death, in the local rhyme :—

> The Lord of Dacres
> Was slain in the North Acres,

fields still known by that name. Many grave mounds remain in Bloody Meadow, where a rude cross leans, half hidden under a tangled hedge ; and in 1848, during some excavations in Saxton churchyard, a stratum of bones, four feet in thickness, was exposed, the poor relics of those who fell in the great fight. Others still are said to have been buried in the little chapel of Lead, a mile away, by the banks of the Cock, whose stream ran red that day. A few stones at the back of Towton Hall mark the place where a votive chapel was erected, where prayers might be said for the souls of the dead, whose numbers on both sides are said by one authority to have reached 36,776. Relics

LEAD CHAPEL.

have been found on the battle-field. Many years ago a wandering antiquary found a farmer's wife breaking sugar with a battle-axe discovered in the river. She did not know what it was, but he did, and secured it. It is now at Alnwick Castle. In 1785 was found a gold ring which had belonged to the Earl of Northumberland, who was carried mortally wounded from the field. It weighs an ounce, and bears the Percy Lion, with inscription, " Now ys thus." Another interesting and pathetic find was a spur, engraved with " En loial amour, tout mon coer," the relic of some unknown knight.

XIV

It is a wild, weird kind of country upon which we enter, on the way from Brotherton to Aberford and the North. Away to the left suddenly opens a wide valley, in an almost sheer drop from the road, looking out upon illimitable perspectives. Then comes Fairburn, followed by what used to be Peckfield Turnpike, where the " Boot and Shoe " inn stands at the fork of the roads, and where the Leeds and London " Royal Mail," " Rockingham," and " Union Post " coaches turned off. Micklefield, two miles beyond, approached by a fine avenue of elms, is an abject coal-mining village, and hauling-gear, smoke, and the inky blackness of the roads emphasise the fact, even if the marshalled coal-wagons on the railway did not give it insistence. Coming up the craggy rise out of Micklefield and its coal, on to Hook Moor, one of the finest stretches of the road, *quâ* road, brings the traveller past the lodge-gates of Parlington Park and the oddly ecclesiastical-looking almshouses beyond, down into the stony old village of Aberford, which lies in a depression on the Cock Beck. Beyond the village, on journeying towards it, one sees the long straight white road ascending the bastioned heights of windy Bramham Moor ; and the sight clinches any half-formed inclination to rest awhile at Aberford before climbing to that airy eminence.

Aberford still seems to be missing its old posting and coaching traffic, and to be awaiting the return of the days when the Carlisle and Glasgow mail changed at the " Swan," a fine old inn, now much shrunken from its original state. Stone-quarrying and the neighbouring coal-mines keep the village from absolutely decaying ; but it still lives in the past. The picturesque old settles and yawning fireplaces of the " Swan," and of that oddly-named inn, the " Arabian Horse," eloquent of the habits of generations ago, survive to show us what was the accommodation those old inns provided. If more primitive, it was heartier, and a great deal more comfortable than that of modern hotels.

By the churchyard wall stands part of the old Market Cross, discovered by the roadside and set up here in 1911 ; with the " Plague Stone " in whose water-filled hollow purchasers placed their money, so that the sellers might not risk infection.

A ruined windmill of strange design, perched on the hillside road behind the village, is the best point whence to gain an idea of the country in midst of which Aberford is set. It is boldly undulating country, hiding in the folds of its hills many old-world villages. Chief among them, two miles off the road, is Barwick-in-Elmete—*i.e.* in the elm country—with its prehistoric

RUINED MILL, OVERLOOKING ABERFORD.

mounds and the modern successor of an ancient maypole, set up in the village street by the cross, presented in May 1898 by Major-General Gascoigne, of Parlington Park.

The road two miles out of Aberford reaches that home of howling winds, that most uncomfortable and undesirable place, Bramham Moor. Here, where the Bramham Moor inn stands at the crossing of the Leeds and York road, a considerable traffic enlivened the way until eighty years ago. Since that time the broad roadways in either direction have been empty, except when the hounds meet here in the hunting season, when, for a brief hour, old times seem come again. It was along this cross-road that " Nimrod,"

that classic coaching authority, travelled in 1827, his
eagle eye engaged in criticism of the Yorkshire provincial coaches.

The rustical driver of the Leeds to York stage,

BARWICK-IN-ELMETE.

happily, did not know who his passenger was. Let us
hope he never saw the criticism of himself, his coach and
horses, and everything that was his, which appeared
shortly afterwards in the *Sporting Magazine.* Everything, says " Nimrod," was inferior. The man who
drove (he scorns, you see, to call him a coachman) was

more like a Welsh drover than anything else.   The day
was cold, but he had neither gloves, boots, nor gaiters.
However, he conducted the coach only a ten miles'
stage, and made up with copious libations of gin for the
lack of warm clothing.   On the way he fell to bragging
with his box-seat passenger of the hair's-breadth
escapes he had experienced when driving one of the
Leeds to London opposition coaches ; and " Nimrod,"
complimenting him on the skill he must have shown on
those occasions, he proceeded to give a taste of his
quality, which resulted in his getting the reins clubbed
and   a   narrow   escape   from   being   overturned.
" Nimrod " soon had enough of it, and at the first
opportunity pretended to be ill and went inside, as
being the least dangerous place.   Arriving at Tadcaster,
ten miles from York, the door was opened, and " Please
to remember the coachman " tingled in the ears of the
passengers.   " What now," asked " Nimrod," " are
you going no farther ? "   " No, sir, but ah's goes back
at night," was the Yorkshireman's answer.   " Then
you follow some trade here, of course ? " continued the
great coaching expert.   " No, sir," said a bystander,
" *he has got his horses to clean.*"   Fancy a coachman,
even if only of that inferior kind, who could not be
called anything better than " the man who drove,"—
fancy a coachman seeing to his own horses.   " Nimrod "
was properly shocked at this, and with memories of
coaching nearer London, with stables and yards full of
ostlers and helpers, and the coachmen, their drinking
done, flirting with the Hebes of the bar, could only say,
with a gasp, " Oh ! that's the way your Yorkshire
coaching is done, is it ? "

He then saw his fellow-passengers pull out sixpence
each and give it to the driver, who was not only
satisfied, but thankful.   This also was a novelty.
Coachmen were, in his experience, tipped with florins
and half-crowns, nor even then did they exhibit
symptoms of thankfulness, but took the coin as of
right.   " What am I to do ? " " Nimrod " asked
himself ; " I never gave a coachman sixpence yet, and

I shall not begin that game to-day." So he " chucked " him a " bob," which brought the fellow's hat down to the box of the fore-wheel in gratitude.

With a fresh team and another driver the journey was continued to York. About half-way, the coach stopped at a public-house, in the old style ; the driver got down, the gin bottle was produced, and, looking out of the window, "Nimrod" was surprised to see the man whom he had thought was left behind at Tadcaster. "What, are you here ? " he asked. " Why, yes," answered the man ; " 'tis market-day at York, and ah's wants to buy a goose or two." " Ah," observed " Nimrod," " I thought you were a little in the huckstering line."

XV

BRAMHAM MOOR leads down into Bramham village, past the Park, where a ruined manor-house, destroyed by fire, stands amid formal gardens and looks tragical. The place wears the aspect of romance, and seems an ideal home for the ideal Wicked Squire of Early Victorian novels. Lord Bingley, who built it and laid out the grounds in the time of Queen Anne, was not more wicked than the generality of his contemporaries, but here are all the "properties" with which those novelists surrounded the cynical deceivers of innocence, who stalked in inky cloaks, curly hats, and tasselled riding-boots through their gory pages. Here is Lord Bingley's Walk, an avenue of gigantic beeches where he did not meet the trustful village maiden, as he ought to have done, by all the rules ; here also is the obelisk at the suggestively named Blackfen, whence twelve avenues diverge—where no tattered witch ever cursed him, so far as can be ascertained. Lord Bingley evidently did not live up to the possibilities of the place, or of his station, nor did those who came after him, for no horrid legend is narrated with bated breath in Bramham village, which lies huddled together in the hollow below the park, the world forgetting, and by the world forgot, ever since that leap year, 1408, when on the 29th of February the Earl of Northumberland, rebelling against Henry the Fourth, was defeated and slain by Sir Thomas Rokeby at the battle of Bramham Moor.

Rising steeply out of Bramham and coming to the crest at Moor End, where the road descends long and

MOOR END.

continuously to Wetherby and the river Wharfe, we come to what used to be regarded as the half-way town between London and Edinburgh. The exact spot, where a milestone told the same tale on either face, is, in fact, one mile north, where the " Old Fox " inn stands. This was, of course, the most noted landmark on the long road, and the drovers who journeyed past it never failed to look in at the " Old Fox " and " wet their whistles," to celebrate the completion of half their task. At Wetherby itself the " Angel " arrogated the title of " half-way house," and was the principal coaching inn. It still stands, like its rival, the " Swan

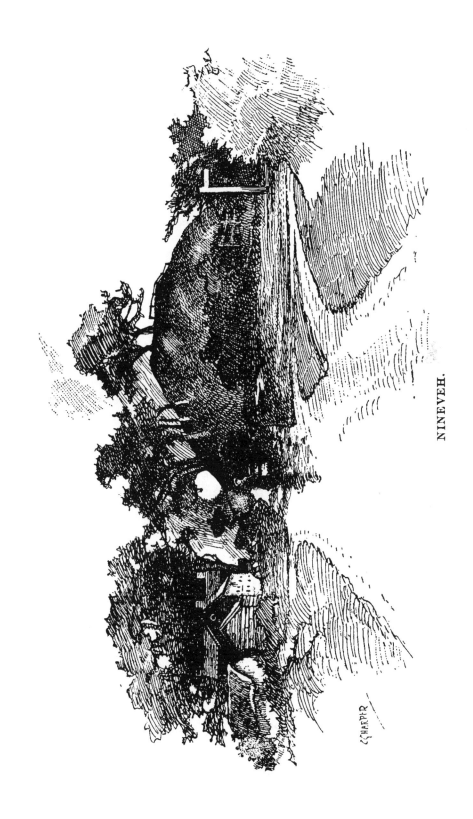

NINEVEH.

and Talbot," smaller than of yore, the larger portion of
its stables now converted into cottages. At the
" Angel " the down London and Glasgow mail dined,
with an hour to spare ; the up coach hurrying through
to its change at Aberford. Wetherby was a change for
the stage-coaches, which ran the whole seventeen miles
to Ferrybridge with the same teams ; a cruelly long and
arduous stretch for the horses.

This is a hard-featured, stony town ; still, as of old,
chiefly concerned with cattle-raising and cattle-dealing,
and crowded on market-days with farmers and drovers
driving bargains or swearing at the terrified efforts of
beasts and sheep to find their way into the shops and
inns. Down on the southern side of the town runs the
romantic Wharfe, between rocky banks, hurrying in
swirling eddies towards its confluence with the Ouse,
below Tadcaster ; and on to the north goes the road,
through the main street, on past the conspicuous spire
of Kirk Deighton church, coming in three miles to
Walshford, where a bridge crosses the rocky, tree-
embowered Nidd, and that old posting-house, the
comfortable-looking " Walshford Bridge Inn," stands
slightly back from the road, looking like a private
mansion gone diffidently into business.

Beyond Walshford Bridge the road turns suddenly
to the left, and, crossing the railway at lonely Allerton
station, passes a substantial red-brick farmhouse which
looks as if it has seen very different days. And indeed
it has, for this was once the " New Inn," a changing-
place for the mails. Now on the right comes the long
wall of Allerton Park, and presently there rises ahead
that strange mound known by the equally strange
name of Nineveh, a tree-crowned hill, partly artificial,
girdled with prehistoric earthworks, and honeycombed
with the graves of the forgotten tribes, to whom it
was probably at once a castle, a temple, and a cemetery.
The road onward to Boroughbridge is, indeed, carried
over a Roman way, which itself probably superseded
the tracks of those vanished people, and led to what is
now the village of Aldborough near Boroughbridge,

once that great Roman city of Isurium which rivalled York itself, and now yields inexhaustible building-stones for modern cottages, and relics that bring the life of those ancients in very close touch with that of our own time : oyster-shells and oyster knives, pomatum-pots, pins, and the hundred little articles in daily use now and fifteen hundred years ago.

Boroughbridge was originally the settlement founded by the Saxons near the ruined and deserted city of Isurium. Afraid of the bogies and evil spirits with which their dark superstitions peopled the ruins, they dared not live there, but built their abiding-place by the river Ure, where the mediæval, but now modernised, village of Boroughbridge stood, and where the bridge built by Metcalf, the blind road- and bridge-maker, over a century ago spans the weedy stream in useful but highly unornamental manner. The battle of Boroughbridge, fought in 1322, is almost forgotten, and coaching times have left their impress upon the town instead. The two chief coaching inns, the " Crown " and the " Greyhounds," still face one another in the dull street ; the " Greyhounds " a mere ghost of its former self, the " Crown " larger, but its stables, where a hundred horses found a shelter, now echoing in their emptiness to the occasional footfall. Oddly enough a medical practitioner, a Dr. Hugh Stott, was landlord of the " Crown " for more than fifty years. Probably he and the landlord of the " Angel " at Ferrybridge were the only two inn-keeping doctors in the kingdom. The " Crown " was anciently the home of the Tancreds, a county family owning property in the neighbourhood : the " Greyhounds " obtains its curious plural from the heraldic shield of the Mauleverers, which displays three greyhounds, " courant." Hotel accommodation was greatly in request at Boroughbridge in the old days ; for from this point branched many roads. Here the Glasgow coaches turned off, and a number of coaches for Knaresborough, Ripon, Harrogate, and the many towns of south-west Yorkshire. The " Edinburgh Express," which went by way of Glasgow, also passed through. Boroughbridge was a busy coaching town, so that ruin, stark, staring, and complete fell upon it when railways came.

The remaining nineteen miles to Northallerton scarce call for detailed description. Kirkby Hill, a mile out of Boroughbridge, lies to the left, its church-tower just within sight. This is followed by the unutterably dull, lifeless, and ugly village of Dishforth, leading to the hamlet of Asenby, where the road descends to the picturesque crossing of the Swale and the Cod Beck, with the village of Topcliffe crowning the ridge on the other side : a village better looking, but as lifeless as the others. Thence flat or gently undulating roads conduct in twelve miles to Northallerton, past Busby Stoop Inn, the villages of Sand Hutton, Newsham, and North and South Otterington.

South Otterington lives with a black mark in the memory of antiquaries as that benighted place where the parishioners thought so little of their church registers some years ago that they allowed the parish clerk to treat all the old ones, dating from before the eighteenth century, as so much waste-paper ; some of them making an excellent bonfire to singe a goose with. They were not singular in this respect, for church-wardens of different places have been known to do the most extraordinary things with these valuable documents. Thoresby, the antiquary, writing of a particular register, remarks that " it has not been a plaything for young pointers. It has not occupied a bacon-cratch or a bread-and-cheese cupboard. It has not been scribbled on, within and without," from which we infer that that was the common fate, and that others *had* been so treated.

The junction of the two main routes of the Great North Road at Northallerton takes place ignominiously outside the goods station at a level-crossing.

After James Pollard.

THE EDINBURGH EXPRESS, 1837.

XVI

THE alternative route now described and North-allerton regained by it, we may resume the long journey to Edinburgh. It is the completest kind of change from the wild ups and downs of the Boroughbridge and Wetherby route to the long featureless stretches that now lie before us. We will not linger in the town, but press onward to where the battle of the Standard, as the battle of Northallerton is often known, was fought, on the right-hand side of the road, near the still unenclosed fragments of Cowton Moor. It was not a great struggle, for the Scots fled after a short resistance, and the great numbers of their slain met their fate rather at the hands of the peasantry, while fleeing through a hostile country, than in combat with the English army.

Standing amid the heathy tussocks of Standard Hill, looking over the Moor, the wide-spreading hill and dale of the Yorkshire landscape fades into a blue or misty distance, and must in its solitude look much the same as it did in those far distant days. Nothing save the name of the hillock and that of the farm called Scot Pits, traditionally said to have been the place where the Scottish dead were buried, remains to tell of the struggle. " Baggamoor," as old chroniclers call the battle-field, from the baggage thrown away by the Scots in their flight, is traversed by the road, which proceeds by way of Oak Tree and Lovesome Hills to Great Smeaton, where the mails changed horses on the short seven miles' stage between it and Northallerton, or the nine miles to Darlington. The "Blacksmith's Arms " was in those times the coaching inn here, but it has long since been converted into cottages. William Tweedie, the last of a succession of three Tweedies who kept the " Blacksmith's Arms " and owed their prosperity to the mails changing at their house, was also the village postmaster. A God-fearing man and an absent-minded, it is recorded of him that during a sermon at the parish church he was surprised in the midst of one of his mental absences by hearing the preacher enlarge upon the text of "Render unto Cæsar." "Ay," he said, in a loud voice, when the duty of paying the king's taxes and just demands was brought home to the congregation, "that puts me in mind o't : there's old Granny Metcalf's bin owin' the matter o' eightpence on a letter these two months past."

Now Widow Metcalf *had* paid that eightpence. She was in church, too. The suddenness of the unjust accusation made her forget time and place, and she retorted with, "William Tweedie, y're a liar ! "

One has a distinct suspicion that by "Lowsey Hill, a small Village contiguous on the Left " (but a place so-named would more properly have been "contagious") mentioned here by Ogilby, he must have meant what is now Lovesome Hill.

The old coach passengers, driving through, or changing at, Great Smeaton must have often wondered, seeing the smallness of the place, what size the neighbouring Little Smeaton, away off to the left, could have been. Their inquiries on that head were usually answered by the coachmen, who were wags of sorts, that Little Smeaton consisted of one dog-kennel and two hen-coops. It is a lonely road between Northallerton and Darlington, and quips of this kind probably tasted better when administered on the spot than they do to the armchair traveller. Particularly lonely is High Entercommon, where a turnpike-gate stood in the days that are done, together with an inn, the "Golden Lion," where a few coaches which made a longer stage from Northallerton changed. Were it not that William Thompson, landlord at the best period in the history of coaching, was a highly reputable person, and had been coachman to Sir Bellingham Graham before he set up as innkeeper, we might point to the house and say how suitable a locality for the secret roadside crimes of old, of which novelists delight to tell ! Roads, and travelling before railways, used to set the romancists busily engaged in spinning the most blood-

curdling stories of villainous innkeepers who, like
Bob Acres, kept " churchyards of their own," and
murderous trap-doors in their guest-rooms giving upon
Golgothas filled with the bones of their many victims.
If one might credit these astounding stories, the inns
that were not murder-shops were few and far between ;
but happily those writers, anxious only to make your
blood creep, were as a rule only exercising their
particularly gory imaginations.

A story of this order is that of a lady who set out in
her carriage to visit some friends in Yorkshire. She had
come to within thirty miles of her destination, when a
thunderstorm which had been threatening broke
violently overhead. Struggling against the elements,
the coachman was glad to espy an old-fashioned
roadside inn presently visible ahead, and, his mistress
expressing a wish to alight and rest until the storm
should abate, he drove up to the door. It was a wild
and solitary spot (they always are in these stories, and
it is astonishing *how* solitary and wild they are, and
how many such places appeared to exist). The rusty
sign creaked dismally overhead, and the window-
shutters flapped violently in the wind on their broken
hinges ; altogether it was not an inviting spot. But
any port in a storm, and so the lady alighted. She was
shown into a large old-fashioned apartment, and the
horses and carriage were stabled until such time as it
might be possible to resume the journey. But, instead
of passing off, the storm grew momentarily worse.
Calling her servant she asked him if it were possible to
continue that night, and on his replying in the negative,
reluctantly resigned herself to staying under a strange
roof. She had her dinner in solitary state, and then
found all the evening before her, with nothing to
occupy the time. She went to the window and looked
out upon the howling storm, and, tired of that
uninviting prospect, gazed listlessly about the room.
It was a large room, ill-furnished, and somewhat out
of repair, for the inn had seen its best days. Evidences
of a more prosperous time were left in the shape of

some scattered articles of furniture of a superior kind and in the presence of a curious piece of ancient tapestry facing her on the opposite wall, bearing a design of a life-sized Roman warrior wielding a truncheon.

But one cannot spend all the evening in contemplating the old chairs and moth-eaten tapestry of a half-furnished room, and the storm-bound traveller soon wearied of those objects. With nothing else to do, she took out her purse and began to count her money and to calculate her travelling expenses. Having counted the guineas over several times and vainly tried to make the total balance properly with her expenditure and the amount she had set out with, she chanced involuntarily to glance across the room. Her gaze fell upon the stern visage of the helmeted Roman, and to her horror the lack-lustre tapestry eyes were now replaced by living ones, intently regarding her and her money. Ninety-nine of every hundred women would have screamed or fainted, or have done both ; but our traveller was evidently the hundredth. She calmly allowed her gaze to wander absent-mindedly away to the ceiling, as if still speculating as to the disposition of the missing odd guineas ; and then, exclaiming, " Ah ! I have it," made for the door, to call her servant, leaving her purse, apparently disregarded, on the table. In the passage outside she met the landlord, who desired to know what it might be she wanted. " To see my man, with orders for the morning," said she. The landlord shuffled away, and her servant presently appeared. She told him what she had observed, and mounting upon the furniture, he examined the tapestry, with the result that he found the wall behind it sound enough in all places, with the exception of the eyes. On pressing the fabric at those points it gave way, disclosing a hole bored through the wall and communicating with some other room. This discovery of course aroused the worst suspicions ; but the storm still raged, it was now late, and to counter-mand the accommodation already secured for the night would be to apprise the landlord of something having been discovered. There was nothing for it but to stay the night. To sleep was impossible, and so the lady, retiring to her bedroom, securely bolting the door, and assuring herself that no secret panel or trap-door existed, sat wakefully in a chair all night. Doubtless the servant did the same, although the story does not condescend to details where he is concerned. At length morning came, without anything happening, and, equally without incident, they set out after breakfast from this place of dread, the lady having previously ascertained that the room on the other side of the wall behind the tapestry was the landlord's private apartment.

These adventures being afterwards recounted, it was called to mind that an undue proportion of highway robberies had for some time past been occurring in the immediate neighbourhood of the inn, and a queer story was remembered of a traveller who had stayed there overnight being robbed soon after leaving by a highwayman, who, without any preliminary parley, desired him to instantly take off his right boot—the boot in which, as a matter of fact, he had stowed away his money. The highwayman, who evidently had been informed of this secret hiding-place, extracted the coin, and, returning the boot, went on his way. It afterwards appeared that the traveller had stowed his money in his boot while under the impression that he was alone in the tapestry-room. He had reckoned without the Centurion.

The inn of course fell into evil repute, and the landlord was soon afterwards compelled to give up business. But the provoking part of it all, from the point of view of the historian, is that the story does not descend to topographical particulars, and that the description of the place . as being in Yorkshire is necessarily of the vaguest, considering the vastness of the shire.

XVII

DALTON-UPON-TEES, three miles onward from High and Low Entercommon, shows little to the passer-by on the Great North Road, who, a mile beyond its scattered cottages, looking as though they had lost themselves, comes to Croft, to the river Tees, and to the end of Yorkshire. It behoves one to speak respectfully of Croft and its Spa, for its waters are as nasty as those of Harrogate, with that flavour of rotten eggs so highly approved by the medical profession, and only the vagaries of fashion can be held accountable for the comparative neglect of the one and the favouring of the other. Sulphur renders both equally nauseous and healthful, but Croft finds few votaries compared with its great and successful rival, and a gentle melancholy marks the spot, where, on the Yorkshire bank, the mouldy-looking Croft Spa Hotel fronts the road, its closed assembly rooms, where once the merry crowds foregathered, given over to damp and mildew.

Croft is in the Hurworth Hunt, and it is claimed by local folk that the Hurworth Country was indicated by " Handley Cross," where Jorrocks and his cronies chased the fox and enjoyed themselves so vigorously. The Spa Hotel was then a place of extremely high jinks. Every night there would be a dinner-party, with much competition as to who could drink the most port or champagne. The test of the sturdiest fellow was to see who could manage to place on his head a champagne or port bottle and lie down and stand up with it still in place. Few reputations, or bottles, survived that ordeal.

But Croft is a pretty place, straggling on both the Yorkshire and Durham banks of the Tees ; with a fine old church commanding the approach from the south. It is worth seeing, alike for its architecture ; for a huge and preposterous monument of one of the Milbankes of Halnaby ; and especially for the extravagantly-

arrogant manorial pew of that family, erected in the
chancel, and elevated in the likeness of two canopied
thrones approached by an elaborate staircase and
over a crimson carpet. This pompous structure dates
from about 1760. The thing would not be credible,
did not we know to what extent the pride and presumption of the old squirearchy sometimes went.

A sturdy old Gothic bridge here carries the road
across the stream into the ancient Palatinate of

CROFT BRIDGE.

Durham. It were here that each successive Prince-
Bishop of that see was met and presented with the
falchion that slew the Sockburn Worm, one of the three
mythical monsters that are said to have infested
Durham and Northumberland. Like the Lambton
Worm, and the Laidly—that is to say, the Loathly—
Worm of Spindleston Heugh, the Sockburn terror,
according to mediæval chroniclers, was a " monstrous
and poysonous vermine or wyverne, aske or werme
which overthrew and devoured many people in fight,
for y^t ye sent of ye poyson was so strong y^t noe p'son
might abyde it." The gallant knight who at some
undetermined period slew this legendary pest was
Sir John Conyers, descended from Roger de Conyers,
Constable of Durham Castle in the time of William
the Conqueror. The family held the manor of Sock-

burn by the curious tenure of presenting the newly
appointed Bishop Palatine of Durham on his first
entry into his diocese with the falchion that slew the
Worm. The presentation was made on Croft Bridge,
with the words :—" My Lord Bishop, I here present
you with the falchion wherewith the champion Conyers

slew the worm, dragon, or fiery flying
serpent which destroyed man, woman
and child ; in memory of which the
king then reigning gave him the manor
of Sockburn, to hold by this tenure,
that upon the first entrance of every
bishop into the county the falchion
should be presented." Taking the
falchion into his hand, the bishop
immediately returned it, wishing the
owner of Sockburn health, long life,
and prosperity, and the ceremony was
concluded. Sockburn, seven miles
below Croft, on the Durham shore of
the Tees, is no longer owned by that
old heroic family, for the proud stock
which in its time had mated with the
noblest in England decayed, and the
last Conyers, Sir Thomas, died a pauper
in Chester-le-Street workhouse in 1810.
The manor-house of Sockburn has
long since been swept away, and
the old church is a roofless ruin,

SOCKBURN
FALCHION.

the estate itself having long since passed to the
Blackett family, in whose possession the wondrous
falchion now remains. The bishops of Durham, no
longer temporal princes, do not now receive it, the last
presentation having been made to Bishop Van Mildert
by the steward of Sir Edward Blackett in 1826.

Croft Bridge, a massive and venerable-looking stone
structure of seven arches, built in 1676, is itself the
successor of a much older building, referred to in a
Royal Brief of 1531 as being " the moste directe and
sure waye and passage for the King o'er Soveraigne

Lorde's armie and ordyn'ce to resort and pass over into the north p'tes and marches of this his reaulme, for the surtie and defence of the same againste the invasion of the Scotts and others his enemyes, over which such armys and ordyn'ces hathe hertofor always bene accostomyed to goo and passe."

Here we are in Durham, and three miles from Darlington. Looking backwards on crossing the bridge, the few scattered houses of the hither shore are seen beside the way ; one of them, the " Comet " hotel, with a weather-beaten picture-sign of the famous pedigree bull of that name, and the inscription, " ' Comet,' sold in 1810 for one thousand guineas." The Tees goes on its rippling way through the pointed arches of the historic bridge, with broad shingly beaches over against the rich meadows, the road pursuing its course to cross that rival stream, the Skerne, at Oxneyfield Bridge, a quarter of a mile ahead. Close by, in a grass meadow to the right of the road, are the four pools called by the terrific name of " Hell's Kettles," which testify by the sulphureous taste of their water to the quality of Croft Spa. Of course, they have their wonderful legends ; Ogilby in 1676 noted that. " At Oxenhall," he says, " are three Pits call'd Hell-kettles, whereof the vulgar tell you many fabulous stories." They have long been current, then ; the first telling how on Christmas Day 1179 the ground rose to the height of the highest hills, " higher than the spires and towers of the churches, and so remained at that height from nine of the morning until sunset. At the setting of the sun the earth fell in with so horrid a crash that all who saw that strange mound and heard its fall were so amazed that for very fear many died, for the earth swallowed up that mound, and where it stood was a deep pool." This circumstantial story was told by an abbot of Jervaulx, but is not sufficiently marvellous for the peasantry, who account for the pool by a tale of supernatural intervention. According to this precious legend, the farmer owning the field being about to carry his hay on June 11, St. Barnabas'

Day, it was pointed out that he had much better
attend to his religious duties than work on the
anniversary of the blessed saint, whereupon he
replied :—

> Barnaby yea, Barnaby nay,
> I'll hae my hay, whether God will or nay :

and, the ground opening, he and his carts and horses
were instantly swallowed up.   The tale goes on to say
that, given a fine day and clear water, the impious
farmer and his carts and horses may yet be seen
floating deep down in these supposedly fathomless
pools !   De Foe, however, travelling this way in 1724,
is properly impatient of these tales.   " 'Tis evident,"
says he, " they are nothing but old coal-pits, filled with
water by the river Tees."

XVIII

DARLINGTON, to which we now come, is a very busy,
very prosperous, very much rebuilt town, nursing a
sub-Metropolitan swagger of architectural pretension in
its chief streets infinitely unlike anything expected by
the untravelled in these latitudes.   There is a distinctly
Holloway   Road—plus   Whitechapel   Road—and
Kennington Lane air about Darlington which does but
add to the piquancy of those streets.   Tumbledown
houses of no great age and no conceivable interest are
shouldered by flaunting shops ; or rather, to speak by
the card, by " stores " and " emporia " ;   these
alternating   with   glittering   public-houses   and
restaurants.   The effect can be paralleled only by
imagining a typical general servant dressed in a skirt
and train for a Queen's Drawing Room, with plough-
boy's boots, a cloth jacket, and ostrich-feathered hat to
complete the costume.   It is a town only now beginning
to realise that prosperity must make some outward
show of the fact, and it is accordingly going in for show
in whole-hearted fashion, and emerging from the grime
in which James the First found it in 1617. " Darneton l"

he said when told its name; " I think it's Darneton i' th' Dirt." Dirty indeed it must have been for James, fresh from his own capital, where they flung their sewage from the windows into the streets, to have found it remarkable. De Foe, fifty years later, said, " Darlington, a post-town, has nothing remarkable in it but dirt, and a high bridge over little or no water." An odd contemporary commentary upon this seems to lurk in the fact that cloth was then brought to Darlington from all parts—even from Scotland—to be bleached !

More akin to those times than these are the names of the streets, which, like those of York, are chiefly " gates " :—High Northgate, Skinnergate, Bondgate, Blackwellgate, and Priestgate.

In vain will the pilgrim seek the " Black Bear," the inn at Darlington to which Frank Osbaldistone, in the pages of *Rob Roy*, came. Scott describes the wayfarers whom the young squire met on his way from London to York and the North as " characters of a uniform and uninteresting description," but they are interesting to us, belonging as they do to a time long past. " Country parsons, jogging homewards after a visitation ; farmers, or graziers, returning from a distant market ; clerks of traders, travelling to collect what was due to their masters in provincial towns ; with now and then an officer going down into the country upon recruiting service." These persons kept the tapsters and the turnpikes busy, and at night time, when they fore-gathered at the roadside inns, sandwiched their talk of cattle and the solvency of traders with terrifying tales of robbers. " At such tales, like children, closing their circle round the fire when the ghost-story draws to its climax, they drew near to each other, looked before and behind them, examined the priming of their pistols, and vowed to stand by each other in case of danger ; an engagement which, like other offensive and defensive alliances, sometimes glided out of remembrance when there was an appearance of actual peril."

This was about 1715. In those days, as Scott says,

H

" journeys of any length being made on horseback, and, of course, by brief stages, it was usual always to make a halt on the Sunday in some town where the traveller might attend divine service, and his horse have the benefit of the day of rest. A counterpart to this decent practice, and a remnant of old English hospitality, was, that the landlord of a principal inn laid aside his character of publican on the seventh day and invited the guests who chanced to be within his walls to take a part of the family beef and pudding."

The " Black Bear " at Darlington, as pictured by Scott, was such a place and the landlord as typical a host, and here Frank Osbaldistone met the first Scot he had ever seen, " a decentish hallion—as canny a North Briton as e'er crossed Berwick Bridge "—which was high praise from mine host, for innkeepers loved not Scottish folk and their thrifty ways. But, as already

S . & . D . R . Nº I . 1825

" LOCOMOTION."

remarked, the " Black Bear " at Darlington does not exist, and coaching relics are rare in this town, whose modern prosperity derives from railways. It is, therefore, with singular appropriateness that Stephenson's " Locomotion," the first engine for that first of railways, the Stockton and Darlington, long since withdrawn from service, has been mounted on a pedestal at Darlington Station. In heathen lands this ancestor of the modern express locomotive would be worshipped as a fetich, and truly it is an ugly and uncanny-looking object.

The Stockton and Darlington Railway Act dates from 1821 ; the line to be worked by " men and horses, or otherwise," steam not being contemplated. The construction was begun in May, 1822, and meanwhile the Rainhill experiments had proved the possibility of locomotive engines. The Act was therefore amended, to authorise the use of them and to

"THE EXPERIMENT."

permit the conveyance of passengers ; a kind of traffic which, odd though it may seem now, was not contemplated by the projectors, whose original idea was a railway for the conveyance of coal. It was on September 27th, 1825, that the line was opened, a train of thirty-eight wagons travelling, as a contemporary newspaper breathlessly announced, " with such velocity that in some parts the speed was frequently twelve miles an hour." Curiously enough, however, the first passengers, after the opening ceremony, were conveyed, not by steam, but by a rough coach, like a gipsy caravan, running on the rails and drawn by a horse. This odd contrivance was called the " Experiment," and did the twelve miles in two hours.   It was followed by other vehicles, consisting of old stage-coach bodies mounted on railway wheels, and it was not until some months had passed that passengers were intrusted to the locomotive.   The first passenger train ran a spirited race with the coach over the twelve miles' course, steam winning by a hundred and twenty yards, amid the cheers of excited crowds.   After thirty-eight years of independent existence, the Stockton and Darlington line was, with its branches, finally absorbed into the North-Eastern system, in 1863.

Darlington is thus a place entirely inimical to coaching interests and memories.   Here, on its pedestal, stands the first of the iron monsters that killed the coaches, and the town itself largely lives by manufacturing railway wagons and iron and steel bridges.   But coaching had had its day, and did not die untimely.   A few years longer and the great high-roads, already inconveniently crowded, must have been widened to accommodate the increased traffic. Railways have been beneficent in many directions, and they have enabled many hundreds of thousands to live in the country who would otherwise have been pent in stuffy streets.   Imagination fails in the task of endeavouring to picture what the roads would have been like to-day if road-travel had remained the only means of communication.   Locomotion would have been immensely restricted, of course ; but the mere increase of population must have brought huge crowds of additional passengers.   Figures are commonly said to be dry, but they can occasionally be eloquent enough.   For instance, when we compare the population of the United Kingdom in 1837, when the Queen came to the throne, and now, and consider the bearing of those figures on this question, they are more than eloquent, and are even startling.   There were twenty-five and a half millions of persons in these islands in the first year of Victoria's reign.   There are now forty-nine millions.   Over twenty-three millions of persons most of whom would have used the roads, added

"I SAY, FELLOW, GIVE MY BUGGY A CHARGE OF COKE, YOUR CHARCOAL IS TOO D——D DEAR."

From an old print.

in eighty years! Of course, the opportunities for cheap and quick travel have made frequent travellers of those who otherwise would never or rarely have stirred from their homes ; but railways have wrought greater changes than that. What, let us think, would have been the present-day position of the city of London without railways ? It must needs have remained largely what it was when the " short stages " conveyed such citizens as did not live in the city to and from their residences in the suburbs, which then extended no further than Highgate, Chiswick, Norwood, and Stockwell. A stage-coach commonly held sixteen persons, twelve outside and four in ; and allowing for those who might manage to walk into the city, how many of such coaches should we require nowadays, supposing railways suddenly abolished, to convey the city's myriad day population ? So many thousands that the task would be impossible. The impossibility of it gives us at once the measure of the railways' might, and raises them from the mere carriers we generally think them to the height of all-powerful social forces whose effects may be sought in every detail of our lives. To them the wide-spreading suburbs directly owe their existence, equally as the deserted main roads of yester-year owed their loneliness to the same cause ; and social scientists have it that they have performed what may at first sight seem a miracle : that, in fact, they have increased the population. If railways had not come to ease the growing pressure that began to be felt upon the roads in the early " twenties," something else must have appeared to do the work of speedy conveyance, and that something would have been the Motor Car. Railway competition and the restrictive legislation that forbade locomotive carriages on highways served to keep motor cars under until recently ; but away back to 1787, when the first steam-carriage was made, the problem of mechanical traction on roads was being grappled with, and many very good steam-cars made their appearance between 1820 and 1830. The caricaturists of the period were

kept busily engaged making more or less pertinent fun
of them ; in itself a testimony to the interest they were
exciting even then.   Here is a typical skit of the period
which takes a renewed interest now that we are on the
threshold of an era of horseless traction.

Few things are more remarkable than the speed with
which railways were constructed through the length
and breadth of the country, but it was long before
through   communication   between   London   and
Edinburgh was established.   It was a coach-guard on
this road who, just before the last coach was run off
it by the locomotive, sadly remarked that " railways
were making a gridiron of England."   They were ;
but it was not until 1846 and 1848, twenty-one and
twenty-three years after the initial success of the
Stockton and Darlington line, that by the opening of
the Edinburgh and Berwick Railway, and the building
of the railway bridge across the Tweed, the last links of
the railway journey between the two capitals were completed.   Even now, it requires the united efforts of
three   entirely   distinct   and   independent   railway
companies to convey the through traffic of under four
hundred miles between the two capitals.   The Great
Northern territory ends at Shaftholme, near Doncaster,
whence the North-Eastern's system conducts to the
Border at Berwick-upon-Tweed, the remaining fifty
miles belonging to the North British Railway.

De Quincey, in his rhapsody on the " English Mail
Coach," says : " The modern modes of travelling cannot
compare with the old mail-coach system in grandeur
and power.   They boast of more velocity, not, however,
as a consciousness, but as a fact of our lifeless know-
ledge, resting upon *alien* evidence ; as, for instance,
because somebody *says* that we have gone fifty miles
in the hour, though we are far from feeling it as a
personal experience, or upon the evidence of a result,
as that actually we find ourselves in York, four hours
after leaving London.   Apart from such an assertion,
or such a result, I myself am little aware of the pace.
But, seated on the old mail-coach, we needed no

evidence out of ourselves to indicate the velocity. We heard our speed, we saw it, we felt it as a thrilling; and this speed was not the product of blind, insensate agencies, that had no sympathy to give, but was incarnated in the fiery eyeballs of the noblest amongst brutes, in his dilated nostrils, spasmodic muscles, and thunder-beating hoofs."

But, in truth, railways and coaches have each their especial variety of the romance of speed. De Quincey missed the quickening rush and contact of the air

THE IRON ROAD TO THE NORTH.

quite as much as any other of the sights, sounds, and sensations he speaks of when travelling by railway; a method of progression which does not admit of outside passengers. Nothing in its special way can be more exhilarating than travelling by coach as an " outside "; few things so unsatisfactory as the position of an " inside "; and if a well-groomed coach is a thing of beauty, there is also a beautiful majesty in a locomotive engine that has been equally well looked after. One of the deep-chested Great Northern expresses puffing its irresistible way past the green eyes of the dropped

semaphores of some busy junction at night-time, or
coming as with the rush and certainty of Fate along the
level stretches of line that characterise the route of the
iron road to the North, is a sight calculated to rouse
enthusiasm quite as much as a coach. Nor are railways
always hideous objects. It is true that in and around
the great centres of population where railway lines
converge and run in filthy tunnels and along smoke-
begrimed viaducts they sound the last note of squalor,
but in the country it is a different matter. The
embankments are in spring often covered with a myriad
wild flowers ; the viaducts give a human interest to
coombe and gully. Lovers of the country can certainly
point to places which, once remote and solitary, have
been populated and spoiled by the readiness of railway
access ; but the locomotive has rendered more holidays
possible, and has kept the roads in a decent solitude for
the cyclist. Imagine, if you please, the Great North
Road nowadays without the railway. A hundred
coaches, more or less, raced along it in the last years
of the coaching age, at all hours of the day and night.
How many would suffice for the needs of the travelling
public to-day ? and what chance would be left to the
tourist, afoot or awheel ?

XIX

BEYOND its grand old church, Darlington has nothing
of great antiquity to show the stranger, save one object
of very high antiquity indeed, before whose hoary age
even Norman and Early English architecture is
comparatively a thing of yesterday. This is the
Bulmer Stone, a huge boulder of granite, brought by
glacial action in some far-away ice-age from the heights
of Shap Fell in distant Westmoreland to the spot on
which it has ever since rested. Darlington has
meanwhile risen out of the void and lonely countryside ;
history has passed by, from the remote times of the
blue-stained Britons, down to the present era of the

blue-habited police; and that old stone remains beside the road to the North. Modern pavements encircle it, and gas-lamps shame with their modernity its inconceivab'e age, but not with too illuminating a ray, and the stranger roaming Darlington after nightfall has barked his shins against the unexpected bulk of the Bulmer Stone, just as effectually as countless generations before him have done.

The long rise of Harrowgate Hill conducts out of Darlington and leads on to Coatham Mundeville, a tiny hamlet on the crest of a hill, with an eighteenth-century house, a row of cottages, and an inn, making together an imposing figure against the sky-line, although when reached they are commonplace enough. The village of Aycliffe lies beyond, on its height, overlooking a scene of quarrying and coal-mining; an outlook which until Cromwell's time was one of dense oak-woods. He it was who caused those woods to be felled to mend the road on to Durham and make it firm enough for his ordnance to pass. Whether the name of Aycliffe derives (as some would have it) from " oak hill," or whether it was originally " High Cliffe," or obtains its name from some forgotten *haia*, or enclosure on this eminence, let us leave for others to fight over : it is an equally unprofitable and insoluble discussion. As well might one hope to obtain a verbatim report of one or other of the two Synods held here in 782 and 789, of which two battered Saxon crosses in the churchyard are thought to be relics, as to determine this question.

For the rest, Aycliffe is quite unremarkable. Leaving it, and coming downhill over an arched crossing over a marsh, dignified by the name of Howden Bridge, we reach Traveller's Rest and its two inns, the " Bay Horse " and " Gretna Green Wedding Inn." An indescribable air of romance dignifies these two solitary inns that confront one another across the highway, and form all there is of Traveller's Rest. The " Wedding Inn," the more modern of the two, has for its sign the picture of a marriage ceremony in that famous Border smithy. The " Bay Horse " is the original Traveller's

Rest. Dating back far into the old coaching and posting times, its stables of that era still remain ; but what renders the old house particularly notable is its

TRAVELLER'S REST.

sign, the odd figure of a horse within an oval, seen on its wall, with the word "Liberty" in company with the name of "Traveller's Rest" and the less romantic than commercial announcement of " Spirituous Liquors." Once, perhaps, painted the correct tint of a " bay " horse, the elements have reduced it to an unobtrusive brown that bids fair to modestly fade into the obscurity of a neutral tint, unless the landlord presently fulfils his intention, expressed to the present historian, of having it repainted, to render it " more viewly " ; which appears to be the North-country phrase for making a thing " more presentable." To this old sign belongs the legend of a prisoner being escorted to Durham Gaol and escaping through the horse ridden by his mounted guard throwing its rider near here. Hence the word " Liberty."

Woodham, a mile distant down the road, bears a name recalling the times when it was in fact a hamlet in those oak woods of which we spoke at Aycliffe. It is now just a group of two or three cottages and a humble inn, the " Stag," in a dip of the way. Beyond it comes Rushyford Bridge, a pretty scene, where a little tributary of the Skerne prattles over its stony bed and disappears under the road beside that old-time posting-house and inn, the " Wheatsheaf." The old house still stands and faces down the road ; but it has long since ceased to be an inn, and, remodelled in recent taste, is now a private residence. The old drive up to the house is now converted into lawns and flower-beds. Groups of that graceful tree, the black poplar, overhang the scene and shade the little hamlet that straggles down a lane to the left hand. The old " Wheatsheaf "

RUSHYFORD BRIDGE.

has its memories. It was a favourite resort of Lord Eldon's. Holt, the landlord, was a boon companion of his. The great lawyer's vacations were for many years spent here, and he established a cellar of his own in the house, stocked chiefly with " Carbonell's Fine Old Military Blackstrap Newcastle Port," of which, although they were decidedly not military, he and his host used to drink seven bottles a day between them, valiant topers that they were. On Saturdays—we have it on the authority of Sydney Smith—they drank eight bottles ; the extra one being to fortify themselves against the Sunday morning's service. Lord Eldon invariably attended church at Rushyford, and compelled his unwilling host to go with him. In London he rarely went, remarking when reproached that he, a buttress of the church, should fail in his devotions, that he was "only an outside buttress."

Lord Eldon was a mean man. It is a defect to be noticed in many others who, like him, have acquired wealth by great personal efforts; with him, however, it reached a height and quality not frequently met. He was not merely " stingy," but mean in the American sense of the word. Contemporary with Fox, Pitt, Sheridan, and other valiant " four-bottle men " of a century ago, and with an almost unlimited capacity for other persons' port, his brother, Lord Stowell, aptly said of him that " he would take any *given* quantity."

With these memories to beguile the way we come to Ferryhill, a mining village crowning a ridge looking over Spennymoor and the valley of the Wear. To Ferryhill came in 1634 three soldiers—a captain, a lieutenant, and an ensign—from Norwich on a tour and in search of adventure. These were early days for tours; days, too, when adventures were not far to seek. However, risky though their trip may have been, they returned in safety, as may be judged from the lieutenant having afterwards published an account of their wanderings through twenty-six English counties. Clad in Lincoln green, like young foresters, they sped the miles with jest and observations on the country they passed through. Of Ferryhill they remark that " such as know it knows it overtops and commands a great part of the country." On this Pisgah, then, they unpacked their travelling plate and " borrowed a cup of refreshing health from a sweet and most pleasant spring "; by which it seems that there were teetotallers in those days also. Those were the days before coal-mines and blast-furnaces cut up the country, and before Spennymoor, away on the left, was converted from a moorland into a township; a sufficiently startling change.

Seen from down the road looking southwards, Ferryhill forms an impressive coronet to . the long ridge of hill on which it stands; its rough, stone-built cottages—merely commonplace to a nearer view—taking an unwarranted importance from the

FERRYHILL: THE ABANDONED ROAD-WORKS.

bold serrated outlines they present against the sky, and looking like the bastioned outworks of some Giant Blunderbore's ogreish stronghold. The traveller from the south, passing through Ferryhill and looking backwards from the depths of the valley road, is cheated of a part of this romantic impression ; he has explored the arid and commonplace village and has lost all possibility of illusion. Let us, therefore, envy the pilgrims from the north. It is, indeed, a highly interesting view, looking back upon Ferryhill, and one touched with romance of both the gentle and the terrifying sort. In the first place, to that tall embankment seen in the accompanying drawing of the scene belongs a story. You perceive that earthwork to be unfinished. It sets out from the cutting seen in the distant hillside, and, crossing the road which comes in a breakneck curve downhill, pursues a straight and level course for the corresponding rise on the hither side, stopping, incomplete, somewhat short of it. " An abandoned railway," thinks the stranger, and so it looks to be ; but it is, in fact, a derelict enterprise embarked upon at the close of the coaching era by a local Highway Board for the purpose of giving a flat and straight road across the valley. It begins with a long cutting on the southern side of the hill on which the village stands, and, going behind the back of the houses, emerges as seen in the picture. The tolls authorised would have made the undertaking a paying one, only road travel ceased before the work was finished. Railways came to put an end to the project and to inflict upon the projectors a ruinous loss.

A more darkling romance, however, broods upon the scene. Away on the western sky-line stands the conspicuous tower of Merrington church, and near it the farmhouse where, on January 28, 1685, Andrew Mills, a servant of the Brass family, who then farmed the adjacent land, murdered the three children in the absence of their parents. It is a story of whose shuddering horror nothing is lost in contemporary accounts, but we will leave it to the imagination.

It is sufficient to say that the assassin, a lad of eighteen years of age, seems to have been half-witted, speaking of having been instigated to the deed by a demon who enjoined him to " Kill—kill." To be more or less mad was no surety against punishment in those times, and

MERRINGTON CHURCH.

so Andrew Mills was found guilty and hanged. Justice seems to have been devilish then, for he was cut down and hanged in chains, after the fashion of the time, beside the road. The peculiar devilry of the deed appears in the fact that he was not quite dead, and survived in his iron cage on the gibbet for days. His sweetheart brought him food, but he could not eat, for every movement of his jaw caused it to be pierced with an iron spike. So she brought milk instead, and so sustained the wretched creature for some time. Legends still recount how he lingered here in agony, his cries by day and night scaring the neighbouring cottagers from their homes, until the shrieks and groans at length ceased, and death came to put an end to his sufferings. The site of the gibbet was by the Thinford inn, near the head of the embankment. The gibbet-post lasted long. Known as " Andrew Mills' Stob," its wood was reputed of marvellous efficacy for toothache, rheumatism, heartburn, and indeed as wide a range of ailments as are

cured by any one of the modern quack medicines that
fill the advertisement columns of our newspapers in
this enlightened age.   It was a sad day for Ferryhill
and the neighbourhood when the last splinter of
Andrew Mills' gibbet was used up, and what the
warty, scrofulous, ulcerous, and rheumaticky inhabitants did then the imagination refuses to consider.

XX

THE surrounding districts anciently possessed a prime
horror (which has lost nothing in the accumulated
legends of centuries) in the " Brawn of Brancepeth."
This terror of the countryside, resolved into plain
matter of fact, seems to have been a wild boar.   Boars
were " brawns " in those days, and the adjacent
" Brancepeth " is just " brawn's path," as Brandon is
supposed to have been " brawn den."   This, to modern
ideas, not very terrible wild animal, seems to have
thoroughly alarmed half a county :—

> He feared not ye loute with hys staffe,
> Nor yet for ye knyghte in hys mayle,
> He cared no more for ye monke with hys boke,
> Than the fyendis in depe Croix Dale.

It will be seen by the last line in this verse that the
author was evidently prepared to back the devil and
all his works against anything the Church could do.
But that is a detail.   The wild boar was eventually
slain by Hodge of the Ferry, who ended him by the
not very heroic process of digging a deep pit in the
course of his usual path, and when the animal fell in,
cutting his head off, doubtless from a safe point of
vantage above.   Divested of legendary trappings,
we can readily picture the facts : the redoubtable
Hodge hiding in the nearest and tallest tree until the
wild boar came along and fell into the hole, when the
champion descended and despatched him in safety.

The traditional scene of this exploit is half a mile to the east of Ferryhill, at a farmstead called Cleve's Cross.

Croixdale, or, as modern times have vulgarised its name, Croxdale, lies on our way to Durham, past the hills of High and Low Butcher Race. Now a shabby roadside village, with a railway station of that name on the main line of the North Eastern Railway, this neighbourhood has also had its romance. The road descends steeply to the river Wear, and in the vicinity

ROAD, RAIL, AND RIVER: SUNDERLAND BRIDGE.

is the dark hollow which mediæval superstition peopled with evil spirits, the " fyendis " who, as the ballad says, cared nothing for the monk with his book. To evict these hardy sprites a cross was erected, hence " Croixdale "; but with what result is not stated.

The cross roads here, too, have their story, for Andrew Tate, a highwayman, convicted of murdering and robbing seven persons near Sunderland Bridge, was hanged where they branch off, in 1602, and afterwards buried beneath the gallows. Now that no devils or highwaymen haunt the lovely woodland borders of the Wear at this spot, it is safe to linger by Sunderland Bridge, just below Croxdale, where the exceedingly picturesque old stone bridge of four arches carries the road over the river. Perhaps the distant railway viaduct may spoil the sylvan solitude of the place, but, on the other hand, it may help to emphasise it. Across that viaduct rush and roar the expresses to and from London and the North ; while the fisherman plys his contemplative craft from the sandy beaches below the bridge. Many a wearied coach passenger, passing this spot in the old days on summer evenings, must have longingly drunk in the beauty of the scene. Other passengers by coach had a terrible experience here in 1822, when the mail was overturned on the bridge and two passengers killed.

Thoresby, in his *Diary*, under date of May 1703, describes one of his journeys with his usual inaccuracy as to the incidence of places, and mentions Sunderland Bridge, together with another, close by. This would be Browney Bridge, to which we come in a quarter of a mile nearer Durham ; only Thoresby places it the other way, where, on the hillside, such a bridge would be impossible. He mentions seeing the legend, " Sockeld's Leap, 1692," inscribed on one of the coping-stones, and tells how two horsemen, racing on this road, jumped on the bridge together with such force that one of them, breaking down the battlements of the bridge, fell into the stream below, neither he nor his horse having any injury.

Ascending the steep rise beyond Browney Bridge, Farewell Hall on the left is passed, the place taking its name, according to the commonly received story, from the Earl of Derwentwater bidding farewell to his friends here when on his way, a captured rebel, to London and the scaffold, in 1715. Climbing one more ridge, the first view of Durham Cathedral is gained on coming down the corresponding descent, a long straight run into the outskirts of the city. Durham Cathedral appears, majestic against the sky, long before any sign of the city itself is noted ; a huge bulk dominating the scene and dwarfing the church of St. Oswald at the foot of the hill, itself no inconsiderable building. To the right hand rises Nine Tree Hill, with

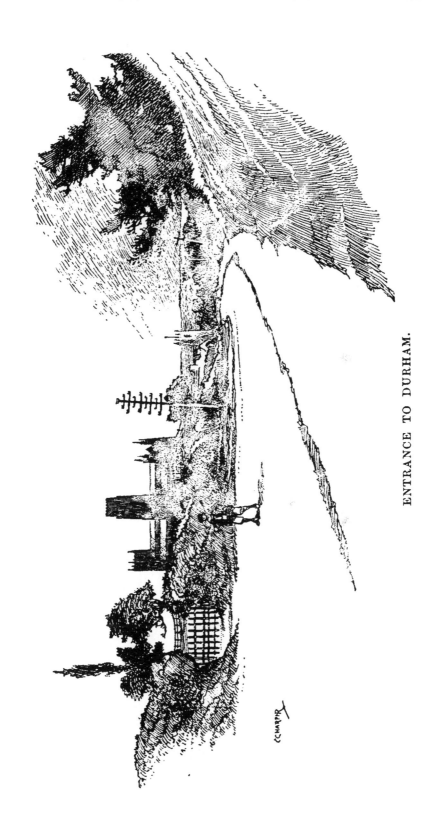

ENTRANCE TO DURHAM.

the nine trees that stand sponsors to it still weirdly conspicuous on its crest, and down beneath it spread the grimy and unkempt works of the Old Elvet Colliery.

XXI

THE traveller pursuing his northward way comes into Durham by the back door, as it were, for the suburb of Old Elvet through which the Great North Road conducts to the ancient city is one of the least prepossessing of entrances, and, besides being dirty and shabby, is endowed with a cobble-stoned road which, as if its native unevenness were not sufficient, may generally be found strewed with fragments of hoop-iron, clinkers, and other puncturing substances calculated to give tragical pauses to the exploring cyclist who essays to follow the route whose story is set forth in these pages. Old Elvet is in no sense a prepossessing suburb of Durham, but its steep and stony street is a true exemplar of the city's other highways and byways, which are nothing if not breakneck and badly paved, as well as being badly kept. But facing Old Elvet's long street is still to be found the " Three Tuns," where coach passengers in the closing years of that era delighted to stay, and where, although the well-remembered hostess of the inn has been gathered to Abraham's bosom, the guest on entering is still served in his bedroom with the welcoming glass of cherry-brandy which it has for the best part of a century been the pleasing custom of the house to present. No other such ambrosial cup as this, rare in itself and hallowed by old memories, greets the wayfarer along the roads nowadays.

From here, or other headquarters, let us set forth to explore the city, planted on a craggy site looking down upon the encompassing Wear that flows deep down between rocky banks clothed thickly with woods. To enter the city proper from " Old Elvet," one must needs cross Elvet Bridge, still narrow, although the subject of a widening by which its width was doubled in 1805. How the earlier coaches crossed it is therefore something of a problem.

It has often been claimed for Durham that it is " the most picturesque city in England," and if by that contention we are to understand the site of it to be meant, the claim must be allowed. Cities are not so many that there is much difficulty in estimating their comparative charms ; and were it even a question of towns, few might be found to have footholds of such beauty.

The Wear and that rocky bluff which it renders all but an island, seemed to the distracted monks of Lindisfarne, worn out with a century's wandering over the north of England in search of safety from the marauding heathen Danes who had laid waste the coast and their island cathedral, an ideal spot ; and so to the harsh necessities of over nine hundred years ago we owe both this selection of a site and the building upon it of a cathedral which should be an outpost for the Lord in the turbulent North and a castle for the protection of his servants. It was in the year 995 that, after a hundred and twenty years of constant wandering, the successors of those monks who had fled from Lindisfarne with the body of their revered bishop, the famous Saint Cuthbert, came here, still bearing his hallowed remains. Their last journey had been from Ripon. Coming near this spot, the Saint, who though by this time dead for over three hundred years, was as masterful as he had been in life, manifested his approval of the neighbourhood by refusing to be carried any further. When the peripatetic bishop and monks found that his coffin remained immovable they fasted and prayed for three days, after which disciplinary exercise, one of their number had a vision wherein it was revealed to him that the Saint should be carried to Dunholme, where he was to be received into a place of rest. So, setting forth again, distressed in mind by not knowing where Dunholme lay, but hoping for a supernatural guidance, they came presently to " a place surrounded with rocks, where there was a river of rapid waves and fishes of various kinds mingling with the floods. Great forests grew there, and in deep valleys were wild animals of many sorts, and deer innumerable." It was when they were come to this romantic place that they heard a milkmaid calling to her companion, and asking where her cow was. The answer, that "she was in Dunholme" was "an happy and heavenly sound to the distressed monks, who thereby had intelligence that their journey's end was at hand, and the Saint's body near its resting-place." Pressing onward, they found the cow in Dunholme, and here, on the site of the present Cathedral, they raised their first " little Church of Wands and Branches." The Cathedral and the Castle that they and their immediate successors raised have long since been replaced ; but the great Norman piles of rugged fane and stern battlemented and loopholed fortress crowning the same rocky heights prove that those who kept the Church anchored here had need to watch as well as pray, to fight secular battles as well as wage war against the devil and all his works. It was this double necessity that made the bishops of Durham until our own time bishops-palatine ; princes of the State as well as of the Church, and in the old days men of the sword as well as of the pastoral staff ; and their cathedral shadows forth these conditions of their being in no uncertain way. There is no finer pile of Norman masonry in this country than this great edifice, whose central tower and east end are practically the only portions not in that style, and of these that grand and massive tower, although of the Perpendicular period, is akin to the earlier parts in feeling ; nor is there another quite so impressive a tower in England as this, either for itself or in its situation, with the sole exception of " Boston Stump," that beacon raised against the sky for many miles across the Lincolnshire levels.

Woods and river still surround the Cathedral, as Turner shows in his exquisite view from the Prebend's

DURHAM CATHEDRAL FROM PREBEND'S BRIDGE.   A ter J. M. W. Turner, R.A.

Bridge, one among many other glorious and unexpected glimpses which the rugged nature of Durham's site provides from all points, but incomparably the best of all. It is here that, most appropriately, there has been placed a decorative tablet, carved in oak, and bearing the quotation from Sir Walter Scott, beginning—

> Half House of God, half Castle ; 'gainst the Scot :

a quotation that gains additional point from the circumstance of the battle of Neville's Cross having been fought against the invading Scots, October 17th, 1346, within sight from the Cathedral roofs. This view is one of Turner's infrequent topographically accurate works. Perhaps even he felt the impossibility of improving upon the beauty of the scene.

Still, annually, after evensong on May 29th, the lay clerks and choristers of the Cathedral ascend to the roof of the great central tower, in their cassocks and surplices, and sing anthems. The first, Farrant's " Lord, for Thy tender mercies' sake," is a reference to the national crime of the execution of Charles the First, and is sung facing south. The second, " Therefore with angels and archangels," by V. Novello, expressing the pious sentiment that the martyred king shall rest in Paradise, in company with those bright beings, is sung facing east ; and the third, " Give Peace in our time, O Lord," by W. H. Callcott, facing north.

The origin of this observance was the thanksgiving for the victory of Neville's Cross, a famous and a complete success, when fifteen thousand Scots were slain and David the Second, the Scottish king and many of his nobles, captured. It was to the special inter-vention of St. Cuthbert, whose sacred banner was carried by Prior John Fossor to Maiden Bower, a spot overlooking the battlefield, that this signal destruction of the enemy was ascribed. The Prior prayed beside it, but his monks are said to have offered up their petitions from the more distant, and safer, vantage-point of the Cathedral towers. Perhaps they had a turn of agnosticism in their minds; but, at any rate, they took no risks.

The original tower-top *Te Deum* afterwards sung on the anniversary seems to have been discontinued at the Reformation. The revival came after the King's Restoration in 1660, when the day was altered to May 29th, to give the celebration the character of a rejoicing at the return of Charles the Second. This revival itself fell into disuse in the eighteenth century, being again restored in 1828, and continued ever since.

The battlefield of Neville's Cross lies to the west of the Cathedral, so no singing takes place on the western side of the tower. The popular, but mistaken, idea in Durham is that this is because a choir-boy once over-balanced on that side and fell from the tower.

If you would see how Castle and Cathedral are situated with regard to the busy modern city, there is no such place as the railway station, whence they are seen dominating the mass of houses, among the smoke-wreaths of commerce, like the martyrs of old steadfast amidst their burning faggots. If again, reversing the order of precedence as seen in the view from Prebend's Bridge, you would have the Castle in the forefront and the Cathedral behind, it is from the Framwellgate Bridge, carrying the Great North Road over the Wear, that another lovely glimpse is seen, ranging to Prebend's Bridge itself.

XXII

BUT time grows short, and we have not long to linger at Durham. Much else might be said of the Cathedral ; of Saint Cuthbert's Shrine, and of the vandal Wyatt, who " restored " the Cathedral in 1775, cutting away, in the process, a depth of four inches from the stonework of much of the exterior. The work cost £30,000, and resulted in eleven hundred tons weight of stone chippings being removed from the building. If that

THE SANCTUARY KNOCKER.

" restorer " had had his way, he would have destroyed
the beautiful Galilee Chapel that projects from the
west front, and forms so uniquely interesting a feature
of Late Norman work.   His idea was to drive a carriage
road round this way.   The work of destruction had,
indeed, already been begun when it was stopped by
more reverent men.

A curious relic still remains upon the door of the
Cathedral's north porch, in the form of a huge knocker,
dating back to Norman times.   Cast in the shape of a
grinning monster's head, a ring hanging from its jaws,
it is the identical sanctuary knocker of Saint Cuthbert's
Sanctuary, which was in use from the foundation of the
Cathedral until 1524.   All fugitives, whatever their
crimes, who succeeded in escaping to Durham, and
reaching the bounds of " Saint Cuthbert's Peace," were
safe   from   molestation   during   thirty-seven   days.
A criminal, grasping the ring of this knocker, could not
be torn from it by his pursuers, under pain of their
being subjected to excommunication ; and lest there
should be bold spirits whom even this could not
affright, there were always two monks stationed, day
and night, in a room above the porch, to watch for
fugitives.   When admitted, the criminal confessed his
crime, with every circumstance attending it, his con-
fession being taken down in writing, in the presence of
witnesses ; a bell ringing in the Galilee tower all the
while, giving notice that some one had fled to the
protection of Saint Cuthbert.   After these formalities,
the fugitive was clothed with a black gown, bearing a
yellow cross on the left shoulder : the badge of the
Saint whose protection he had secured.   After the
days of grace had expired, and in the event of no
pardon being obtained, ceremonies were gone through
before the Shrine, in which the malefactor solemnly
forswore his native land for ever.   Then, safeguarded
to the coast, he was shipped out of the kingdom by
the first vessel sailing after his arrival.

There must have been many an exciting chase along
the roads in those times, and many a criminal who richly

DURHAM CASTLE AND CATHEDRAL FROM BELOW FRAMWELLGATE BRIDGE.

deserved punishment must have escaped it by the very skin of his teeth. Many another, no doubt, was seized and handed over to justice, or slain, on the threshold of safety. Other fugitives still—and here Saint Cuthbert appears in better guise—victims of hatred and oppression, private or political, claimed the saintly ægis, and so escaped the vengeance of their enemies. So, looking upon the ferociously grinning mask of the knocker, glaring with eyeless sockets upon Palace Green, we can reconstruct the olden times when, at his last gasp, the flying wretch seized the ring and so came into safety. By night, the scene was more impressive still, for there were crystals in those sockets then, and a lamp burning behind, so that the fugitive could see his haven from afar, and make for it.

To-day, Saint Cuthbert avails no man, as the county gaol and the assize courts sufficiently prove, and Durham city is essentially modern, from the coal-grit that powders its dirty streets to the awfully grotesque effigy of a Marquis of Londonderry that lends so diabolical an air to the Market-place, where the Statute Fair is held, and where he sits, a coal-black effigy across his coal-black horse, towering over the steam merry-go-rounds, like Satan amid the revelries of a Walpurgis Night. This bronze effigy is probably the most grotesque statue in the British Isles, and loses nothing of that quality in the noble Marquis being represented in a hussar uniform with flying dolman over his shoulders, and a busby, many sizes too large for him, on his head, in an attitude as though ferociously inviting the houses on the other side of the street to " come on."

That diarising Scotswoman, Mrs. Calderwood of Coltness, travelling south in 1756, wrote :—

" We dined at Durhame, and I went to see the cathedrall ; it is a prodigious bulky building. It was on Sunday betwixt services, and in the piazzas there were several boys playing at ball. I asked the girl that attended me, if it was the custome for the boys to play at ball on Sunday : she said, ' they play on other

κ

days, as well as on Sundays.' She called her mother to show me the church ; and I suppose, by my questions, the woman took me for a heathen, as I found she did not know of any other mode of worship but her own ; so, that she might not think the Bishop's chair defiled by my sitting down in it, I told her I was a Christian, though the way of worship in my country differed from hers. In particular, she stared when I asked what the things were that they kneeled upon, as they appeared to me to be so many Cheshire cheeses."

FRAMWELLGATE BRIDGE.

They were hassocks : articles apparently then not known to Presbyterians.

And so she continued southward :—

" Next day, the 7th, we dined none, but baited at different places, and betwixt Doncaster and Bautry a man rode about in an odd way, whom we suspected for a highwayman. Upon his coming near, John Rattray pretended to make a quarle with the post boy, and let him know that he keept good powder and ball to keep such folks as him in order ; upon which the felow scampered off cross the common."

The Great North Road leaves Durham over

Framwellgate Bridge, built by Bishop Flambard in Norman times. Although altered and repaired in the fifteenth century and later, it is still substantially the same bridge. There was once a fortified gateway on it, but that was taken down in 1760. Bridge, River, Castle, and Cathedral here form a majestic picture.

XXIII

AND now to take the open road again. The chief features of the road between Durham and Newcastle are coal-pits, dismal pit villages, and coal-dust. Not at once, however, is the traveller introduced to these, and the ascent out of Durham, through the wooded banks of Dryburn, is very pretty. It is at Framwellgate Moor, a mile and a half from the city, that the presence of coal begins to make itself felt, in the rows of unlovely cottages, and in the odd figures of the pitmen, who may be seen returning from their work, with grimy faces and characteristic miner's dress. Adjoining this village, and undistinguishable from it by the stranger, is the roadside collection of cottages known as " Pity Me," taking its name from the hunted fox in the sign of the " Lambton Hounds " inn.

Framwellgate is scarce left behind before there rises up in the far distance, on the summit of one of the many hills to the north-east, a hill-top temple resembling the Athenian Acropolis, and as you go northward it is the constant companion of your journey for some seven or eight miles. This is " Penshaw Monument," erected on that windy height in 1844, four years after his death, to the memory of John George Lambton, first Earl of Durham. It cost £6,000, and commemorates the championship of the Reform movement in its earlier and precarious days by that statesman. Like many another monument, impressive at a distance, a near approach to it leads to disillusion, for its classic outlines are allied to coarse workmanship, and its eighteen great

columns are hollow.   Penshaw, deriving its name from
Celtic words, signifying a wooded height, still has its
woodlands to justify the name given nearly a thousand
years ago.

The little town of Chester-le-Street lies three miles
ahead, past the few cottages of Plawsworth, once the
site of a turnpike-gate, and by Chester Moor and the
pretty wooded hollow of Chester Dene, where the

PENSHAW MONUMENT.

Con Burn goes rippling through the undergrowth to
join the river Wear, and a bridge carries the highway
across the gap.   Approaching Chester-le-Street, the
bright yellow sandstone mass of Lumley Castle, the
ancient seat of the Earl of Scarborough, is prominent
in the valley to the right, while beyond it rise the
woods of Lambton Castle, the Earl of Durham's
domain.   The neighbourhood of Chester-le-Street yet
preserves the weird legend of the " Lambton Worm,"
and Worm Hill is still pointed out as the home of that
fabulous monster who laid the country under con-
tribution for the satisfying of his voracious appetite,
and was kept in good humour by being provided with
the milk of nine cows daily.   Many had essayed to slay
the serpent and had fallen victims instead, until the
heir of Lambton, returned from the red fields and
hair's-breadth escapes of foreign wars, set forth to free
the countryside from the terror.   But before he
started, he was warned (so the legend runs), that unless

he vowed, being successful in his enterprise, to slay the first living thing he met on his return, the lords of Lambton would never, for nine generations to come, die in their beds. He took that vow, and, armed with his trusty sword and a suit of armour made of razor-blades, met and slew the Worm, who coiled himself round the knight in order to crush him as he had the others, and so was cut in pieces against the keen edges. But the victor on returning was met by his father, instead of by the favourite dog who had been destined for the sacrifice. The sword dropped from his nerveless hand, and he broke the vow. What mattered it where the future generations died; in their beds, or, as warriors might wish, in their boots?

As a matter of fact, the next nine heirs of Lambton *did* die more or less violent deaths; a circumstance which is pointed to in proof of the legend's truth. If other proof be wanting, one has only to visit Lambton Castle, where the identical trough from which the Worm drank his daily allowance of milk is still shown the curious tourist!

Chester-le-Street bears little in its appearance to hint at its great age and interesting history. A very up-to-date little town, whose prosperity derives from its position as a marketing centre for the surrounding pitmen, it supports excellent shops and rejoices in the possession of Co-operative Societies, whose objects are to provide their subscribers with whatever they want at cost price, and to starve the trader, who trades for profit, out of existence. That shops and societies exist side by side, and that both look prosperous, seems remarkable, not to say miraculous. Let the explanation of these things be left to other hands.

The name of Chester-le-Street doubly reveals the Roman origin of the place from the castle on the road which existed here in those distant times, and has easily survived the name of Cunecaster, which the Saxons gave it. At Cunecaster the ancient bishopric of Bernicia, forerunner of the present See of Durham, had its cathedral for a hundred and thirteen years, from A.D. 882 to 995 ; having been removed from the Farne Islands on the approach of the heathen Danes, the monks carrying the coffin of their sainted bishop, St. Cuthbert, with them on their wanderings. The dedication of the present church to Saints Mary and Cuthbert is a relic of that time, but the building itself is not older than the thirteenth century. It preserves an ancient anchorites' cell.

The finest surviving anchorage in England is this of Chester-le-Street. It is built against the north wall of the tower, and is of two storeys with two rooms on each. Two " low-side " windows communicating with the churchyard remain, and a smaller opening into the church is close by. Through this, food and offerings were passed to the anchorite, together with the keys of the church treasure-chest, left in his custody by the clergy. From this orifice the holy hermit could obtain a view all over the building, and an odd hagioscope or " squint," pierced through one of the pillars, allowed of his seeing the celebration of Mass at a side-chapel, in addition to that at the High Altar. This was no damp and inconvenient hermitage, for when the anchorite was kicked out at the Reformation, and bidden go and earn an honest living, his old home was let to three widows. Eventually, in 1619, the curate found the place so desirable—or, as a house-agent would say, so " eligible "—that he took up his abode there.

The church also contains fourteen monumental effigies ascribed, without much truth in the ascription, to the Lumleys. John, Lord Lumley, collected them from ruined abbeys and monasteries in the neighbourhood some three hundred years ago, and called them ancestors. He was technically right ; for we all descend from Adam, but not quite so right when, finding he could not steal a sufficient number of these " ancestors," he commissioned the local masons to rough-hew him out a few more. They are here to this day, and an ill-favoured gang they look, too.

The town of Chester-le-Street found little favour

with De Foe, who, passing through it, found the place
" an old dirty thoroughfare town." The modern
traveller cannot say the same, but it is possible that
if he happened to pass through on Shrove Tuesday,
he would describe the inhabitants as savages ; for on
that day the place is given up to a game of football
played in the streets, the town taking sides, and
when the ball is not within reach, kicking one another.
With a proper respect for their shop fronts, the trades-
folk all close on this day.

The three miles between Chester-le-Street and
Birtley afford a wide-spreading panorama of the
Durham coal-field. Pretty country before its mineral
wealth began to be developed, its hills and dales reveal
chimney-shafts and hoisting-gear in every direction,
and smoke-wreaths, blown across country by the raging
winds of the north, blacken everything. Birtley is a
typical pit village and its approaches characteristic of
the coal country. The paths are black, the hedges and
trees ragged and sooty, and tramways from the collieries
cross the road itself, unfenced, the trucks dropping coal
in the highway. One coal village is as like another as
are two peas. They are all frankly unornamental ;
all face the road on either side, each cottage the exact
replica of its unlovely neighbour, and the footpaths are
almost invariably unpaved. These are the homes of
the " Geordies," as the pitmen once were invariably
called. They were rough in their ways, but very
different from the more recent sort : the trade-unionist
miner : the better educated but more discontented
and unlovable man. But " Geordie," the old-type
typical pitman, was not a bad fellow, by any
means. If any man worked, literally, by the sweat of
his brow, it was he, in his eight hours' shift down in the
stifling tunne's of the coal-mine. He earned a high
wage and deserved a higher, for he carried his life in his
hand, and any day that witnessed his descent half a
mile or so into the black depths of the pit might also
have seen an accident which, by the fall of a roof of
coal, by fire or flood, explosion, or the unseen but

deadly choke-damp, should end his existence, and that of hundreds like him.

The midday aspect of a coal village is singularly quiet and empty. Scarce a man or boy is to be seen. Half of them are at work down below, in the first day shift to which they went at an early hour of the morning : and those of the night, who came up when the others descended, are enjoying a well-earned repose. A coal-miner just come to bank from his coal-hewing, looks anything but the respectable fellow he generally is, nowadays. With his peaked leathern cap, thick short coat, woollen muffler, limp knickerbockers, blue worsted stockings, heavy lace-up boots and dirty face, he looks like a ha'f-bleached nigger football-player. When washed, his is a pallid countenance which the stranger, unused to the colourless faces of those who work underground, might be excused for thinking that of one recovering from an illness. And washing is a serious business with " Geordie." Every pitman's cottage has its tub wherein he " cleans " himself, as he expresses it, while the women-folk crowd the street. What the cottages lack in accommodation they make up for in cleanliness and display. The pitman's wife wages an heroic and never-ending war against dirt and grime, and both have an astonishing love of finery and bright colours which reveals itself even down to the door-step, coloured a brilliant red, yellow, or blue, according to individual taste. Nowadays football claims " Geordie's " affections before anything else. That rowdy game, more than any other, serves to work off any superfluous energy, and there are stories, more or less true, which tell of pitmen, tired of waiting for " t' ball," starting " t' gaame " by kicking one another instead ! Coursing, dog-fancying, and the breeding of canaries are other favourite pitmen's pastimes, and they dearly love a garden. Where an outdoor garden is impossible, a window garden is a favourite resource, and even the ugliest cottages take on a certain smartness when to the yellow doorstep are added bright green window-shutters and a window full of scarlet

THE COAL COUNTRY.

geraniums. Very many pitmen are musical. We do not in this connection refer to the inevitable American organ whose doleful wails wring your very heart-strings as you pass the open cottage doors on Sunday afternoons, but to the really expert violinists often found in the pit villages.

XXIV

AT Harlowgreen Lane, where a little wayside inn, the "Coach and Horses," stands beside a wooded dingle, we have the only pleasant spot before reaching

A WAYSIDE HALT.　　　*After Rowlandson.*

Gateshead. Prettily rural, with an old-world air which no doubt gains an additional beauty after the ugliness of Birtley, it looks like one of those roadside scenes pencilled so deftly by Rowlandson, and might well have been one of the roadside stopping-places mentioned in that book so eloquent of the Great North Road, Smollett's *Roderick Random*. No other work gives us so fine a description of old road travel, partly founded, no doubt, upon the author's own observation of the wayfaring life of his time. Smollett himself travelled from Glasgow to Edinburgh and London in 1739, and in the character of Roderick he narrates some of his own adventures. For a good part of the way Roderick found neither coach, cart, nor wagon on the road, and so journeyed with a train of pack-carriers so far as Newcastle, sitting on one of the horses' pack-saddles. At Newcastle he met Strap, the barber's assistant, and they journeyed to London together, sometimes afoot; at other times by stage-wagon, a method of travelling which, practised by those of small means, was a commonplace of the period at which Smollett wrote. It was a method which had not changed in the least since the days of James the First, and was to continue even into the first years of the nineteenth century. Fynes Morrison, who wrote an *Itinerary*—and an appallingly dull work it is—in the reign of the British Solomon, talks of them as " long covered wagons, carrying passengers from place to place ; but this kind of journeying is so tedious, by reason they must take wagon very early and come very late to their innes, that none but women and people of inferior condition travel in this sort." Hogarth pictured these lumbering conveyances, which at their best performed fifteen miles a day, and Rowlandson and many other artists have employed their pencils upon them.

Smollett is an eighteenth-century robust humorist, whose works are somewhat strong meat for our times ; but he is a classic, and his works (unlike the usual run of " classics," which are aptly said to be books which no one ever reads) have, each one, enough humour to furnish half a dozen modern authors, and are proof against age and change of taste. To the student of bygone times and manners, *Roderick Random* affords (oh! rare conjunction) both instruction and amusement. It is, of course, a work of fiction, but fiction based on personal experience, and palpitating with the life of the times in which it was written. It thus affords a splendid view of this great road about 1739, and of the way in which the thrifty Scots youths then commonly came up to town.

Their first night's halt was at a hedgerow alehouse, half a mile from the road, to which came also a pedlar. The pedlar, for safety's sake, screwed up the door of the bedroom in which they all slept. " I slept very sound," says Roderick, " until midnight, when I was disturbed by a violent motion of the bed, which shook under me with a continual tremor.   Alarmed at this phenomenon, I jogged my companion, whom, to my amazement, I found drenched in sweat, and quaking through every limb ; he told me, with a low, faltering voice, that we were undone, for there was a bloody highwayman with loaded pistols in the next room ; then, bidding me make as little noise as possible, he directed me to a small chink in the board partition, through which I could see a thick-set, brawny fellow, with a fierce countenance, sitting at a table with our young landlady, having a bottle of ale and a brace of pistols before him."   The highwayman was cursing his luck because a confederate, a coachman, had given intelligence of a rich coach-load to some other plunderer, who had gone off with £400 in cash, together with jewels and money.

" But did you find nothing worth taking which escaped the other gentleman of the road ? " asked the landlady.

" Not much," he replied. " I gleaned a few things, such as a pair of pops, silver-mounted (here they are) ; I took them, loaded, from the charge of the captain who had charge of the money the other fellow had taken, together with a gold watch which he had concealed in his breeches. I likewise found ten Portugal pieces in the shoes of a Quaker, whom the spirit moved to revile me, with great bitterness and devotion ; but what I value myself mostly for is this here purchase, a gold snuff-box, my girl, with a picture on the inside of the lid, which I untied out of the tail of a pretty lady's smock."

Here the pedlar began to snore so loudly that

the highwayman heard him through the partition.
Alarmed, he asked the landlady who was there, and
when she told him, travellers, replied, " Spies ! you
jade ! But no matter, I'll send them all to hell in an
instant."

The landlady pacified him by saying that they were
only three poor Scotchmen ; but Strap by this time
was under the bed.

The night was one of alarms. Roderick and Strap
awakened the pedlar, who, thinking the best course
was not to wait for the doubtful chance of being
alive to see the morning dawn, vanished with his
pack through the window.

After having paid their score in the morning, the
two set out again. They had not gone more than
five miles before a man on horseback overtook them,
whom they recognised as Mr. Rifle, the highwayman
of the night before. He asked them if they knew
who he was. Strap fell on his knees in the road.
" For heaven's sake, Mr. Rifle," said he, " have mercy
on us, we know you very well."

" Oho ! " cried the thief, " you do ! But you shall
never be evidence against me in this world, you
dog ! " and so saying, he drew a pistol and fired at
the unfortunate shaver, who fell flat on the ground,
without a word. He then turned upon Roderick, but
the sound of horses'· hoofs was heard, and a party of
travellers galloped up, leaving the highwayman barely
time to ride off. One of them was the captain who
had been robbed the day before. He was not, as may
already have been gathered, a valiant man. He turned
pale at the sight of Strap. " Gentlemen," said he,
" here's murder committed ; let us alight." The
others were for pursuing the highwayman, and the
captain only escaped accompanying them by making his
horse rear and snort, and pretending the animal was
frightened. Fortunately, Strap " had received no
other wound than what his fear had inflicted " ; and
after having been bled at an inn half a mile away, they
were about to resume their journey, when a shouting

crowd came down the road, with the highwayman in the midst, riding horseback with his hands tied behind him. He was being escorted to the nearest Justice of the Peace. Halting a while for refreshment, they dismounted Mr. Rifle and mounted guard, a circle of peasants armed with pitchforks round him. When they at length reached the magistrate's house, they found he was away for the night, and so locked their prisoner in a garret, from which, of course, he escaped.

Roderick and Strap were now free from being detained as evidence. For two days they walked on, staying on the second night in a public-house of a very sorry appearance in a small village. At their entrance, the landlord, who seemed a venerable old man, with long grey hair, rose from a table placed by a large fire in a neat paved kitchen, and, with a cheerful countenance, accosted them with the words : " *Salvete, pueri ; ingredimini.*" It was astonishing to hear a rustic landlord talking Latin, but Roderick, concealing his amazement, replied, " *Dissolve frigus, ligna super foco large reponens.*" He had no sooner pronounced the words than the innkeeper, running towards him, shook him by the hands, crying, " *Fili mi dilectissime ! unde venis ?—a superis, ni fallor.*" In short, finding them both read in the classics, he did not know how to testify his regard sufficiently ; but ordered his daughter, a jolly, rosy-cheeked damsel, who was his sole domestic, to bring a bottle of his *quadrimum* , repeating at the same time from Horace, " *Deprome quadrimum Sabinâ, O Thaliarche, merum diota.*" This was excellent ale of his own brewing, of which he told them he had always an *amphora*, four years old, for the use of himself and friends.

The innkeeper proved to be a schoolmaster who was obliged, by his income being so small, to supplement it by turning licensed victualler. He was very inquisitive about their affairs, and, while dinner was preparing, his talk abounded both with Latin tags and with good advice to the inexperienced against the deceits and wickedness of the world. They fared sumptuously on roast fowl and several bottles of *quadrimum*, going to bed congratulating themselves on the landlord's good-humour. Strap was of opinion that they would be charged nothing for their lodging and entertainment. "Don't you observe," said he, "that he has conceived a particular affection for us ; nay, even treated us with extraordinary fare, which, to be sure, we should not of ourselves have called for ? "

Roderick was not so sanguine. Rising early in the morning, and having breakfasted with their host and his daughter on hasty-pudding and ale, they desired to know what there was to pay.

'Biddy will let you know, gentlemen," said the old rascal of a tapster, "for I never mind these matters. Money-matters are beneath the concern of one who lives on the Horatian plan : *Crescentem sequitur cura pecuniam.*"

Meanwhile, Biddy, having consulted a slate that hung in a corner, gave the reckoning as eight shillings and sevenpence.

"Eight shillings and sevenpence ! " cried Strap ; "'tis impossible ! You must be mistaken, young woman."

"Reckon again, child," said the father very deliberately ; "perhaps you have miscounted."

"No, indeed, father," replied she. "I know my business better."

Roderick demanded to know the particulars, on which the old man got up, muttering, "Ay, ay, let us see the particulars : that's but reasonable " ; and, taking pen, ink, and paper, wrote :

	s.	d.
To bread and beer, ...	0	6
To a fowl and sausages, ...	2	6
To four bottles of quadrim, ...	2	0
To fire and tobacco, ...	0	7
To lodging, ...	2	0
To breakfast, ...	1	0
	8	7

As he had not the appearance of a common publican, Roderick could not upbraid him as he deserved, simply

remarking that he was sure he had not learned from
Horace to be an extortioner. To which the landlord
replied that his only aim was to live *contentus parvo*, and
keep off *importuna pauperies*.

Strap was indignant. He swore their host should
either take one-third or go without; but Roderick,
seeing the daughter go out and return with two stout
fellows, with whom to frighten them, thought it politic
to pay what was asked.

It was a doleful walk they had that day. In the
evening they overtook the wagon, and it is here,
and in the following scenes, that we get an excellent description of the cheap road travel of
that era.

Strap mounted first into the wagon, but retired,
dismayed, at a tremendous voice which issued from
its depths, with the words, " Fire and fury! there
shall no passengers come here." These words came
from Captain Weazel, one of the most singular
characters to be found in Smollett's pages.

Joey, the wagoner, was not afraid of the captain,
and called out, with a sneer: " Waunds, coptain,
whay woan't you soofer the poor wagoneer to meake a
penny? Coom, coom, young man, get oop, get oop;
never moind the coptain."

" Blood and thunder! where's my sword? "
exclaimed the man of war, when the two eventually
fell, rather than climbed, into the wagon's dark
recesses, and incidentally on to his stomach.

" What's the matter, my dear? " asked a female
voice.

" The matter? " replied the captain; " my guts
are squeezed into a pancake by that Scotchman's
hump." The " hump," by the way, was poor Strap's
knapsack.

" It is our own fault," resumed the feminine voice;
" we may thank ourselves for all the inconveniences
we meet with. I thank God I never travelled so
before. I am sure, if my lady or Sir John were to
know where we are, they would not sleep this night

for vexation. I wish to God we had written for the chariot; I know we shall never be forgiven."

"Come, come, my dear," replied the captain, "it don't signify fretting now; we shall laugh it over as a frolic; I hope you will not suffer in your health. I shall make my lord very merry with our adventures in the diligence."

The unsophisticated lads were greatly impressed by this talk. Not so the others. "Some people," broke

TRAVELLERS ARRIVING AT AN INN.

After Rowlandson.

in another woman's voice, "give themselves a great many needless airs; better folks than any here have travelled in wagons before now. Some of us have rode in coaches and chariots, with three footmen behind them, without making so much fuss about it. What then! we are now all on a footing; therefore let us be sociable and merry. What do you say, Isaac? Is not this a good motion, you doting rogue? Speak, old Cent. per cent.! What desperate debt are you thinking of ? What mortgage are you planning ? Well, Isaac, positively you shall never gain my favour till you turn over a new leaf, grow honest, and live like a gentleman. In the meantime, give me a kiss, you old fool."

The words, accompanied by hearty smack, enlivened the person to whom they were addressed to such a degree, that he cried, in a transport, though with a faltering voice : " Ah, you baggage ! on my credit you are a waggish girl—he, he, he ! " This laugh introduced a fit of coughing which almost suffocated the poor usurer—for such they afterwards found was the profession of their fellow-traveller.

At their stopping-place for the night they had their first opportunity of viewing these passengers. First came a brisk, airy girl, about twenty years of age, with a silver-laced hat on her head instead of a cap, a blue stuff riding-suit, trimmed with silver, very much tarnished, and a whip in her hand. After her came, limping, an old man, with a worsted night-cap buttoned under his chin and a broad-brimmed hat slouched over it, an old rusty blue cloak tied about his neck, under which appeared a brown surtout that covered a thread-bare coat and waistcoat, and a dirty flannel jacket. His eyes were hollow, bleared, and gummy ; his face shrivelled into a thousand wrinkles, his gums destitute of teeth, his nose sharp and drooping, his chin peaked and prominent, so that when he mumped or spoke they approached one another like a pair of nut-crackers ; he supported himself on an ivory-headed cane, and his whole figure was a just emblem of winter, famine, and avarice.

The captain was disclosed as a little thin creature, about the age of forty, with a long, withered visage very much resembling that of a baboon. He wore his own hair in a queue that reached to his rump, and on it a hat the size and cock of Antient Pistol's. He was about five feet and three inches in height, sixteen inches of which went to his face and long scraggy neck ; his thighs were about six inches in length; his legs, resembling two spindles or drum-sticks, two feet and a half; and his body the remainder; so that, on the whole, he appeared like a spider or grasshopper erect. His dress consisted of a frock of bear-skin, the skirts about half a foot long, a hussar waistcoat, scarlet breeches reaching half-way down his thighs, worsted stockings rolled up almost to his groin, and shoes with wooden heels at least two inches high; he carried a sword very nearly as long as himself in one hand, and with the other conducted his lady, who seemed to be a woman of his own age, still retaining some remains of good looks, but so ridiculously affected that any one who was not a novice in the world would easily have perceived in her deplorable vanity the second-hand airs of a lady's woman.

This ridiculous couple were Captain and Mrs. Weazel. The travellers all assembled in the kitchen of the inn, where, according to the custom of the time, such impecunious wayfarers were entertained; but the captain desired a room for himself and his wife, so that they might sup by themselves, instead of in that communal fashion. The innkeeper, however, did not much relish this, but would have given way to the demand, providing the other passengers made no objection. Unhappily for the captain's absurd dignity, the others *did* object; Miss Jenny, the lady with the silver-trimmed hat, in particular, observing that " if Captain Weazel and his lady had a mind to sup by themselves, they might wait until the others should have done." At this hint the captain put on a martial frown and looked very big, without speaking; while his yoke-fellow, with a disdainful toss of her nose, muttered something about " creature ! " which Miss Jenny overhearing, stepped up to her, saying, " None of your names, good Mrs. Abigail. Creature ! quotha —I'll assure you—no such creature as you, neither—no quality-coupler." Here the captain interposed, with a " D——n me, madam, what do you mean by that ? "

" Sir, who are you ? " replied Miss Jenny; " who made you a captain, you pitiful, trencher-scraping, pimping curler ? The army is come to a fine pass when such fellows as you get commissions. What, I suppose you think I don't know you ? You and your helpmate are well met : a cast-off mistress and a bald valet-de-chambre are well yoked together."

"Blood and wounds!" cried Weazel; "d'ye question the honour of my wife, madam ? No man in England durst say so much—I would flay him, carbonado him! Fury and destruction! I would have his liver for my supper !" So saying, he drew his sword and flourished it, to the great terror of Strap ; while Miss Jenny, snapping her fingers, told him she did not value his resentment that !

We will pass over the Rabelaisian adventures of the night, which, amusing enough, are too robust for these pages ; and will proceed to the next day's journey. Before they started, Weazel had proved himself the arrant coward and braggart which the reader has already perceived him to be ; but, notwithstanding this exposure, he entertained the company in the wagon with accounts of his valour : how he had once knocked down a soldier who had made game of him ; had tweaked a drawer by the nose who had found fault with his picking his teeth with a fork ; and had, moreover, challenged a cheesemonger who had had the presumption to be his rival.

For five days they travelled in this manner. On the sixth day, when they were about to sit down to dinner, the innkeeper came and told them that three gentle-men, just arrived, had ordered the meal to be sent to their apartment, although told that it had been bespoken by the passengers in the wagon,—to which information they had replied : " The passengers in the wagon might be d——d ; their betters must be served before them ; they supposed it would be no hardship on such travellers to dine on bread and cheese for one day."

This was a great disappointment to them all, and they laid their heads together to remedy it, Miss Jenny observing that Captain Weazel, being a soldier by profession, ought to protect them. The captain adroitly excused himself by saying that he would not, for all the world, be known to have travelled in a wagon ; swearing, at the same time, that, could he appear with honour, they should eat his sword sooner than his provision. On this declaration, Miss Jenny, snatching his weapon, drew it and ran immediately into the kitchen, where she threatened to put the cook to death if he did not immediately send the victuals into their room. The noise she made brought the three strangers down, one of whom no sooner perceived her than he cried, " Ha ! Jenny Ramper ! what brought thee hither ? "

" My dear Jack Rattle," she replied, running into his arms, " is it you ? Then Weazel may go whistle for a dinner—I shall dine with you."

They consented with joy to this proposal ; and the others were on the point of being reduced to a very uncomfortable meal, when Joey, the wagoner, understanding the whole affair, entered the kitchen with a pitchfork in his hand, and swore he would be the death of any man who should pretend to seize the victuals prepared for the wagon. On this, the three strangers drew their swords, and, being joined by their servants, bloodshed seemed imminent ; when the landlord, interposing, offered to part with his own dinner, for the sake of peace ; which proposal was accepted and all ended happily.

When the journey was resumed in the afternoon, Roderick chose to walk some distance beside the wagoner, a merry, good-natured fellow, who informed him that Miss Jenny was a common girl of the town, who, falling in company with a recruiting officer who had carried her down in the stage-coach from London to Newcastle, was obliged to return, as her companion was now in prison for debt. Weazel had been a valet-de-chambre to my Lord Fizzle while he lived separate from his lady ; but on their reconciliation she insisted on Weazel's being turned off, as well as the woman who had lived with him : when his lordship,

to get rid of them both with a good grace, proposed
that Weazel should marry his mistress, when he would
procure a commission in the army for him.

Roderick and the wagoner both had a profound
contempt for Weazel, and resolved to put his courage
to the test by alarming the passengers with the cry
of " a highwayman " as soon as a horseman should
appear. It was dusk when a man on horseback
approached them. Joey gave the alarm, and a
general consternation arose ; Strap leaping out of the
wagon and hiding himself behind a hedge ; the usurer
exclaiming dolefully and rustling about in the straw,
as though hiding something ; Mrs. Weazel wringing her
hands and crying ; and the captain pretending to
snore.

This latter artifice did not succeed with Miss Jenny,
who shook him by the shoulder and bawled out :
" 'Sdeath ! captain, is this a time to snore when we are
going to be robbed ? Get up, for shame, and behave
like a soldier and man of honour."

Weazel pretended to be in a great passion for being
disturbed, and swore he would have his nap out if all
the highwaymen in England surrounded him. " What
are you afraid of ? " continued he ; at the same time
trembling with such agitation that the whole vehicle
shook.

" Plague on your pitiful soul ! " exclaimed Miss
Jenny ; " you are as arrant a poltroon as was ever
drummed out of a regiment. Stop the wagon, Joey,
and if I have rhetoric enough, the thief shall not
only take your purse, but your skin also."

By this time the horseman had come up with them,
and proved to be a gentleman's servant, well known
to Joey, who told him the plot, and desired him to
carry it on a little further, by going up to the wagon and
questioning those within. Accordingly he approached,
and in a terrible voice demanded, " Who have we got
here ? " Isaac replied, in a lamentable voice, " Here's
a poor, miserable sinner, who has got a small family to
maintain, and nothing in the world but these fifteen

shillings, which, if you rob me of, we must all starve together."

" Who's that sobbing in the corner ? " continued the supposed highwayman.

" A poor, unfortunate woman," answered Mrs. Weazel, " on whom, I beg you, for Christ's sake, to have compassion."

" Are you maid or wife ? " said he.

" Wife, to my sorrow," said she.

" Who, or what is your husband ? " continued he.

" My husband," continued Mrs. Weazel, " is an officer in the army, and was left sick at the last inn where we dined."

" You must be mistaken, madam," said he, " for I myself saw him get into the wagon this afternoon." Here he laid hold of one of Weazel's legs, and pulled him out from under his wife's petticoats, where he had concealed himself. The trembling captain, detected in this inglorious situation, rubbed his eyes, and affecting to wake out of sleep, cried, " What's the matter ? "

" What's the matter ? The matter is not much," answered the horseman ; " I only called in to inquire after your health, and so adieu, most noble captain." So saying, he clapped spurs to his horse, and was out of sight in a moment.

▶ It was some time before Weazel could recollect himself ; but at length, reassuming his big look, he said, " 'Sdeath ! why did he ride away before I had time to ask him how his lord and his lady do ? Don't you remember Tom, my dear ? " addressing his wife.

" Yes," replied she ; " I think I do remember something of the fellow ; but you know I seldom converse with people of his station."

" Hey-day ! " cried Joey ; " do you know the young man, captain ? "

" Know him ? " cried Weazel ; " many a time has he filled a glass of Burgundy for me at my Lord Trippett's table."

▶ " And what may his neame be, coptain ? " said Joey.

" His name !—his name," replied Weazel, " is Tom Rinser."

" Waunds ! " cried Joey, " a has changed his own neame then ! for I'se lay any wager he was christened John Trotter."

This raised a laugh against the captain, who seemed very much disconcerted ; when Isaac broke silence and said, " It was no matter who or what he was, as he had not proved the robber they suspected. They ought to bless God for their narrow escape."

" Bless God ! " said Weazel, " for what ? Had he been a highwayman I should have eaten his blood and body before he had robbed me or any one in this diligence."

" Ha, ha, ha ! " cried Miss Jenny ; " I believe you will eat all you kill, indeed, captain."

The usurer was so well pleased at the end of this adventure that he could not refrain from being severe, and took notice that Captain Weazel seemed to be a good Christian, for he had armed himself with patience and resignation, instead of carnal weapons, and worked out his salvation with fear and trembling ; whereupon, amidst much laughter, Weazel threatened to cut the Jew's throat. The usurer, taking hold of this menace, said :—" Gentlemen and ladies, I take you all to witness, that my life is in danger from this bloody-minded officer : I'll have him bound over to the peace." This second sneer procured another laugh against the captain, who remained crestfallen for the rest of the journey.

XXV

THE remaining miles to Gateshead are made up of the shabby village of Low Fell, where the road begins to rise, and the uninteresting way over the ridge of the Fell itself. By the word " Fell," North of England people describe what Southerners call a hill. The common land of Gateshead Fell, 675 acres, was enclosed under Acts of Parliament, 1809, 1822.

MODERN NEWCASTLE: FROM GATESHEAD.

Many were the gibbets erected in the old days on Gateshead Fell. The last was that on which swung the body of Robert Hazlett, who on this spot, on the evening of August 6th, 1770, robbed a young lady, Miss Margaret Benson, who was returning to Newcastle in a post-chaise from Durham. On the same night a post-boy was relieved of his bags at the same place. Hazlett was hanged at Durham, and his body gibbeted here, twenty-five feet high. For some time afterwards, every day for an hour, an old man was seen to kneel and pray at the foot of the gibbet. It was the wretched man's father ! A beacon was fixed on the Fell in the winter of 1803-4, on an alarm of invasion ; hence this height was afterwards known as " Beacon Hill."

The present-day aspect of the road does not hint at anything so tragical, and is merely commonplace, the last touch of vulgarity added by the trams that ply along it from Gateshead.

The place-name of Gateshead seemed to John Ogilby, in his book, *Britannia Depicta*, 1676, to require explanation, and he proceeded to say that it was " alias Gate-Side, seated on the Banks of the Tine, by the Saxons call'd Gates-heved, i.e. *Capræ Caput*, or Goat's-head, perchance from an Inn with such a sign."

But perchance not. While the Saxon name certainly was Gatesheved, it meant " road's head," either in allusion to the Roman bridge across the river being broken down and passage being possible only by water, or else referring to the abruptly-descending land on either side, where the road would seem to be coming to a sudden end.

Gateshead is to Newcastle what Southwark is to London, and the Tyne which runs between may be likened in the same way to the Thames. Comparison from any other point of view is impossible. Gateshead is nowadays a great deal worse than it was when Doctor Johnson called it " a dirty lane leading to Newcastle." It may be ranked among the half-dozen dirtiest places on earth, and the lane which the Doctor saw has sent forth miles of streets as bad as itself, so that the geographical distribution of filth and squalor has in modern times become very wide. There are two ways of entering Newcastle since the High Level Bridge across the Tyne has supplemented what used to be the old Tyne Bridge, once, and until fifty years ago, the only way of crossing the river except by boat. When Stephenson flung his High Level Bridge across that stream, as yellow, if not as historic, as the Tiber, he provided a roadway for general traffic beneath the railway, and the old bridge lost its favour, simply for the reason that to cross it the steeply descending West Street and Bottle Lane had to be taken and the just as steeply ascending bank of the river on the Newcastle side to be climbed ; while by the High Level a flat road was provided. It is true that all traffic, pedestrian and wheeled, pays a small toll for the privilege, but it is the lesser of the two evils.

Let those who have no concern with old times take their easeful way through the gloomy portals of the High Level Bridge, eighty-five feet above high-water mark. But let us examine the steep and smelly street, paved with vile granite setts and strewn with refuse, which conducts to the Tyne Bridge, or the Swing Bridge as it is nowadays, since the old structure was removed, the channel of the river deepened, and the wonderful swinging portion of the remodelled bridge, 281 feet in length, and swung open or closed by hydraulic power, constructed in 1876. With that work went the last fragments of the Roman bridge built by Hadrian (*Publius Aelius Hadrianus*) more than a thousand years before ; a bridge which, indeed, gave the Roman camp its name of *Pons Ælii.* His bridge, long in ruins, was replaced in 1248 by a mediæval structure which was destroyed by a flood in 1771.

This way came the coaches, climbing into Newcastle up Sandhill and the Side, whose steep and curving roadway remains to prove how difficult were the ways of travellers as well as transgressors in the old times. Old and new jostle here. The Swing Bridge turns silently on its pivot to the touch of a lever in its signal tower, and a force our grandfathers never knew performs the evolution ; but side by side with this miracle still stand the darkling lanes and steep waterside alleys of Gateshead and Newcastle that were standing before science and commerce, mother and daughter, came down upon the Tyne and transformed it.

A writer in an old-time Northern magazine appears to have been jolted into a bad humour respecting Newcastle's precipitous old approach :—" We have no connection whatever with the coal-trade, and were never at Newcastle but once, passing through it on the top of an exceedingly heavy coach, along with about a score of other travellers. But, should we live a thousand years, it would not be possible for us to forget that transit. We wonder what blockhead first built Newcastle ; for before you can get into and out of it, you must descend one hill and ascend another, about as steep as the sides of a coal-pit. Had the coach been upset that day, instead of the night before and the day after, there would have been no end and, indeed, no beginning, to this magazine. We all clustered as thickly together on the roof of the vehicle (it was a sort of macvey, or fly) as the good people of Rome did to see Great Pompey passing along :—but we, on the contrary, saw nothing but a lot of gaping inhabitants, who were momentarily expecting to see us brought low. We remarked one man fastening his eye upon our legs that were dangling from the roof under an iron rail, who, we are confident, was a *Surgeon.* However, we kept swinging along, from side to side, as if the macvey had been as drunk as an owl, and none of the passengers, we have reason to believe, were killed that day—it was a maiden circuit. But, after all, we love Newcastle, and wish its coals may burn clear and bright till consumed in the last general conflagration."

High over head goes the High Level, and the smoke and rumble of its trains mingle with the clash of Newcastle's thousand anvils and the reek of her million chimneys ; but there still stands against the sky-line—most fittingly seen from the Gateshead

OLD NEWCASTLE : SHOWING THE TOWN BRIDGE, NOW DEMOLISHED CARRYING THE GREAT NORTH ROAD OVER THE TYNE.

After J. M. W. Turner, R.A.

bank at eventide, when petty details are lost and only
broad effects remain—the coroneted steeple of St.
Nicholas and the great black form of the Norman keep,
reminding the contemplative that Monkchester was
the name of the city before the Conqueror came and
built that fortress whose fame as the " New Castle "
has remained to this day to give a title to the place,
just as the " new work " at Newark has ever since
stood sponsor for that town. Again, no sooner have
you crossed the Swing Bridge and come to Quayside
than other vestiges of old Newcastle are encountered,
in the remains of the Castle wall and the steps that
lead upwards to Castle Garth, where shoemakers and
cobblers of footgear of the most waterside and
unfashionable character still blink and cobble in their
half-underground dens, the descendants, probably, of
those whom a French traveller remarked here in the
time of Charles the Second. If, instead of climbing
these stairs, the traveller elects to follow the track
of the coaches, he will traverse Sandhill, which in
very early days was an open space by the river, but
has for centuries past been a street. It was at Sandgate
close by, according to the ballad, that the lassie was
heard to sing the well-known refrain of " Weel may the
keel row, the boat that my love's in," and indeed it is a
district that breathes romance, commonplace though
its modern offices may look. Does not the Moot Hall
look down upon Sandhill ? " Many a heart has broken
inside those walls," said a passer-by, with unwonted
picturesqueness, to the present writer, gazing at that
hall of justice.

There is a pretty flavour of romance—compact, it is
true, of the most unpromising materials, like the
voluptuous scents which modern science extracts
from coal-tar—still clinging to Sandhill. Just where
a group of curious old houses, very old, very tall, and
nearly all windows, remains, the explorer will perceive
a memorial tablet let into one of the frontages, setting
forth that " From one of the windows of this house,
now marked with a blue pane of glass, Bessie Surtees

eloped with John Scott, afterwards Lord Chancellor Eldon, November 18th, 1772." John Scott was twenty-one years of age at the time, and was at home on vacation from Oxford. His father, a successful coal-fitter, had sent him, as he had already done his elder brother, William, afterwards Lord Stowell, to the University. He had already gained a fellowship there, which he forfeited on his elopement with, and marriage to, his Bessie. She descended from her casement by the aid of a ladder hidden by an accomplice in the shop below, and they were over the Border and wedded by the blacksmith at Blackshields before any one could pursue. Bessie's relatives were bitterly opposed to the match, and so, nearly without resources, the pair had to resort to London and live frugally in Cursitor Street while he studied hard at law, instead of, as originally intended, for the Church. His first year's earnings scarce amounted to enough to live on. " Many a time," said he in after years, " have I run down from Cursitor Street to Fleet Market, to buy sixpennyworth of sprats for our supper." The turning-point in his career occurred in a case in which he insisted on a legal point against the wishes of his clients. The case was decided against him, but was reversed on appeal on the point he had contested. From that time continued success awaited him, and he eventually became Lord Chancellor. The dashing Romeo of an earlier day became, however, a very different person in after years. Much poring over parchments and long-continued professional strife took all the generous enthusiasm out of him, and by ways not the most scrupulous he amassed one of the greatest fortunes ever scraped together by a successful lawyer. Bessie, meanwhile, had become quite as much of a handful as she had been an armful.

Romance wanes. As Conservators of the Tyne, the Corporation of Newcastle have, for the last four centuries, proclaimed their authority by once in every five years going in procession on the river, in various craft. It was on these occasions the acknowledged custom that, on returning and landing, the Mayor should choose the prettiest girl in the crowds of spectators and publicly salute her with a civic kiss. In acknowledgment of this favour his Worship presented her with a new sovereign. But the procession of " Barge Day," as it was called, was discontinued after May 16th, 1901, and is not likely to be revived.

From Sandhill the coaches journeyed along the Side, which remains as steep and almost as picturesque as ever, even if not rendered additionally curious by the gigantic railway arch that spans it and clears the roofs of its tallest houses. The last mail-coach left Newcastle for Berwick and Edinburgh, with the Union Jack flying at half-mast, on July 5, 1847, and those days are so thoroughly done with that none of Newcastle's coaching inns are left. Indeed, the whole character of the place has changed since little over a century and a half ago, when John Wesley entered the opinion in his diary that it was a " lovely place and lovely company," and, furthermore, said that " if he were not journeying in hope of a better world, here he would be content to live and die." Coal had even then been shipped for centuries from Newcastle, but miles of manufactories had not yet arisen upon the banks of " coaly Tyne," and so unprogressive was the town that it was still, with gardens and orchards, easily comprised within its mediæval walls; those walls which had many a time withstood the Scots, and even when Wesley was here in 1745 were being prepared to resist the Pretender.

Newcastle—difficult as it may now be to realise the fact—was then a very small town, and was governed accordingly. Primitive punishments as well as primitive government survived until a hundred and fifty years ago, when scolds still wore bridles or were ducked, and when local tipplers yet perambulated the streets in the drunkard's cloak, an ingenious instrument of little ease which now reposes in the Museum.

Far beyond the ancient walls now extend the streets of the modern city; Grey Street chief among them,

M

classically gloomy and extra-classically grimed to the blackness of Erebus; a heavy Ionic pillar at its

'THE DRUNKARD'S CLOAK."

northern end bearing aloft the statue of Earl Grey, the Prime Minister who secured the passing of the first Reform Bill in 1832.

Away from the chief business streets, many of the curious old thoroughfares may be sought, but they are nowadays the receptacles of inconceivable dirt, and anything but desirable. The narrow streets called "chares" answer to the "wynds" of Edinburgh and the "rows" of Yarmouth. Their name has been the subject of jokes innumerable, and misunderstandings not a few; as, when a judge, previously unacquainted with Newcastle, holding an assize here, heard a witness say that he saw "three men come out of the foot of a chare," and ordered him out of the witness-box, thinking him insane, until the jury of Newcastle men explained matters.

Despite its smoke and untidiness, the folks of this grimy Tyneside city have a good conceit of it. To them it is "canny Newcastle," an epithet whose meaning differs from the Scotch, and here means "fine," or "neat." The stranger who fails to find those qualities, who perceives instead the defects of dirt and a pall of smoke that blackens everything to an inky hue, and accordingly thanks Providence that his home is elsewhere, is to the Tynesiders a Goth.

For Newcastle is practical. It has its great newspapers, and has produced literary men of note; but the forging of iron and steel, the shrinking of steel jackets upon big guns, the making of ships and all kinds of munitions of war appeal principally to the Novocastrian who may by chance have no especial love of that coaling trade which is pre-eminently and historically his. It is therefore quite characteristic of Newcastle folks that, in the mid-century, a literary man, since become famous, was as a boy solemnly warned by a townsman against such a career as he was contemplating. " Ah'm sorry," said he, " to hear that ye want to go to London, and to take to this writing in the papers. It'll bring ye to no good, my boy. I mind there was a very decent friend of mine, auld Mr. Forster, the butcher in the Side. He had a laddie just like you ; and nothing would sarve him but he must go away to London to get eddicated, as he called it ; and when he had got eddicated, he wouldn't come back to his father's shop, though it was a first-class business. He would do nothing but write, and write, and write ; and at last he went back again to London, and left his poor old father all alone ; and ah've never heard tell of that laddie since ! "

Of course he had not. What rumours of literary life in London could then have penetrated to the shores of the " coaly Tyne." That laddie, however, was John Forster, the biographer of Dickens.

These practical men of Newcastle have achieved the most wonderful things. The home of the Stephensons was at Wylam, only nine miles away, and so the town can fairly claim the inventor of railways among its natives. We need not linger to discuss the wonders of the locomotive ; they are sufficiently evident. Newcastle men have even changed the character of their river. There are still those who can recollect the Tyne as a shallow stream in which the laden " keels," heaped up with coal, not infrequently grounded. Nowadays the largest war-vessels are built up-stream, at Elswick, and take their stately way to the sea with their heavy armaments, and no mishap occurs. Clanging arsenals and factories line the banks for many more miles than the historian, anxious for his reputation, dare mention. The Armstrong works alone are over a mile long, and employ some sixteen thousand hands. Lord Armstrong himself was the inventor of hydraulic machinery ; and the Swan incandescent electric lamp, which bears the name of its inventor, was the work of a Newcastle man. Others of whom England is proud were born here, notably Admiral Lord Collingwood. To their practicality these men of Newcastle add sentiment, for they have carefully placed tablets on the houses where their celebrated men were born, and they have not only erected a monument to Stephenson, but have also placed one of his first engines—" Puffing Billy "—on a pedestal beside the High Level Bridge, where the huge modern expresses roar past the quaint relic, day and night, in startling contrast. Also, they one and all have the most astonishingly keen affection for their old parish church of St. Nicholas, in these latter days become a cathedral.

If you would touch a Novocastrian on his most sensitive spot, praise or criticise the cathedral church of St. Nicholas, and he will plume himself or lose his temper, as the case may be. That building, and especially its tower, with the wonderful stone crown supported on ribbed arches and set about with its cluster of thirteen pinnacles, is the apple of Newcastle's eye. It figures as a stock decorative heading in the Newcastle papers, and does duty in a hundred other ways. Built toward the close of the sixteenth century, that fairy-like corona has had its escapes, as when, during the stubborn defence in 1644, under the Royalist Sir John Marley, the Scottish general, Alexander Leslie, Lord Leven, commanding the besieging forces, threatened to batter it down with his cannon if the town were not at once surrendered. To this Sir John Marley made the very practical reply of causing all his Scottish prisoners to be placed in the tower, and sent word to the besiegers that they might, if they would, destroy it, but that their friends should perish at the same time. The " Thief and Reiver " bell, a relic of old times when the outlaws of Northumberland were given short shrift wherever and whenever found, is still rung before the opening of the annual fair, and recalls the old custom of giving those

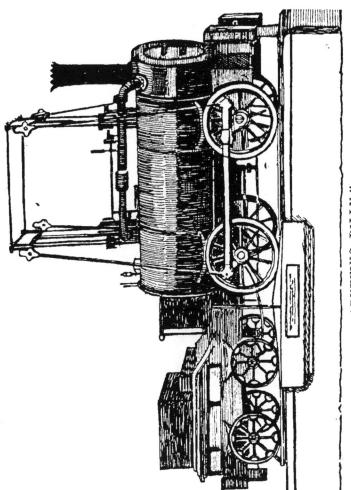

"PUFFING BILLY."

gentry immunity from arrest during fair-time ; but it
would probably not be safe for any one " wanted " by
the police to rely upon this sentimental survival.

XXVI

For fully a mile and a half on leaving Newcastle
the road runs over the Town Moor, a once wild waste of
common, and even now a bleak and forbidding open
space whose horizon on every side commands the gaunt
Northumbrian hills, or is hidden with the reek of
Newcastle town, or the collieries that render the way
sordid and ugly. Newcastle's lovely pleasance,
Jesmond Dene, is hidden away to the right from the
traveller along the road, who progresses through
Bulman's Village (now dignified with the new name of
Gosforth), Salter's Lane, Wide Open and Seaton Burn
with sinking heart, appalled at the increasing
wretchedness and desolation brought by the coal-
mining industry upon the scene. Off to the right lies
Killingworth, among the collieries, where George
Stephenson began his career in humble fashion. His
cottage stands there to this day. At the gates of
Blagdon Park, eight miles from Newcastle, where the
white bulls of the Ridleys guard the entrance in
somewhat spectral fashion, the surroundings improve.
Here the Ridleys have been seated for centuries, and
from their wooded domain watched the belching
smoke of the pits they own, which year by year and
generation by generation have added to their wealth.
Lord Ridley is now the representative of these owners
of mineral wealth, and lord of Blagdon. Midway of the
long park wall that borders the road on the way to
Morpeth stand the modern lodge and gates, erected in
1887 ; with that relic of old Newcastle, the Kale Cross,
just within the grounds and easily seen from the
highway. The building is not so much a cross as a
market-house, and is just a classical pavilion in the

Doric style, open on all sides to the weather. It stood, until the middle of the eighteenth century, upon the Side at Newcastle, and marked the centre of the market then held there. The townfolk presented it to the Matthew White Ridley of the period, and here in lovelier surroundings than it knew originally, it stands, the wreathed urns and couchant lion on its roof contrasting finely with a dense background of foliage.

THE GATES OF BLAGDON PARK

Beyond the park, the road crosses the Black Dene, whence Blagdon derives its name ; one of those ravines that now begin to be a feature of the way. This expands on the right hand into Hartford Dene, to which Newcastle picnic-parties come in summer-time for brief respite from the smoke and clangour of their unlovely town. Thence, through Stannington, Clifton, and Catchburn, and to the long and tortuous descent into Morpeth, lying secluded in the gorge of the Wansbeck.

Morpeth is little changed since coaching times, but the one very noticeable alteration shows by what utter barbarians the town was inhabited towards the close of that era. Entering it, the turbulent Wansbeck is crossed by a stone bridge, built in 1830, to provide better accommodation for the increased traffic than the ancient one, a few yards up stream, afforded. For some five years longer the old building was suffered to remain, and then, with the exception of its piers, it was demolished.   No one benefited by its destruction, it stood in no one's way, and its utility was such that a footbridge, a graceless thing of iron and scantling, has been erected across those ancient piers, to continue the access still required at this point from one bank to the other.   It was to our old friends the monks that travellers were beholden for that ancient Gothic bridge, and their old toll-house still remains, after having passed through a varied career as a chapel, a school, and a fire-engine house.   Turner's view shows the road over the bridge, looking south ; with the castle gate-house on the hill-top, a great deal nearer than it actually is.   This, the sole relic of that old stronghold, has in later years been restored until it looks almost as new as the would-be Gothic of the gaol, which stands beside the modern bridge on entering the town and deludes the more ignorant into a belief of its genuine antiquity.   At Morpeth, until the assizes were removed to Newcastle, justice was dispensed in this sham mediæval castle, built in 1821, and now, all too vast for present needs, used as a police-station.   The old town gaol, at the other end of the town, facing the market-place, is much more interesting.   Built in the likeness of a church tower, curfew is still rung from its belfry, beneath the queer little figures on the roof.   Market-day brings crowds of drovers and endless droves of sheep and cattle to this spot, to say nothing of the pigs, singularly plentiful in these parts.   " He's driving his swine to Morpeth market," is an expression still used of a snoring man in the neighbourhood.   Always excepting market-day, Morpeth is now a curiously quiet and dreamy town.   The stress of ancient times has left its few relics in the mouldering remains of strong and defensible walls, and in certain proverbs and sayings reflecting discreditably upon the Scottish people, but the seventeenth and eighteenth centuries

MORPETH.

After J. M. W. Turner, R.A.

are more evident in its streets than previous eras.
To those centuries belong the many old inns with signs
for the most part redolent of the coaching age : the
" Nag's Head," the " Grey Nag's Head," the " Queen's
Head," " Turk's Head," and " Black Bull " ; this last
with an odd semi-circular front and a beautiful coach-
entrance displaying some fine Adam decoration.

That Morpeth folk still cherish old anti-Scottish
sayings is not at all remarkable ; for old manners, old
sayings, and ancient hatreds die slowly in such places as
this, and moreover, the Morpeth of old suffered terribly
from Scottish raiders. Later times saw a more peaceful
irruption, when Scottish youths came afoot down the
great road in quest of fame and fortune in the south.
People looked askance upon them as Scots, while
innkeepers hated them for their poverty and their
canniness. Those licensed victuallers thought, with
Dr. Johnson, who did not greatly like them either, that
" the finest prospect for a Scotchman was the high road
that led him into England." This bitter satire, by the
way, was in reply to a Mr. Ogilvie, who had been
contending on behalf of the " great many noble wild
prospects " which Scotland contained. Smollett, in his
Humphry Clinker, shows how greatly the Scots were
misliked along this route about 1766. He says that,
from Doncaster northwards, *all* the windows of *all*
the inns were scrawled with doggerel rhymes in abuse of
the Scottish nation. This fact was pointed out to
that fine Scottish character, Lismahago, and with it a
particularly scurrilous epigram. He read it with some
difficulty, the glass being dirty, and with the most
starched composure.

" Vara terse and vara poignant," said he ; " but with
the help of a wat dishclout it might be rendered more
clear and parspicuous."

The country between Morpeth and Alnwick is dotted
with peel-towers and their ruins, built in the wild old
times when the ancestors of these peaceful Scots came in
quest of spoil, laying waste the Borders far and wide.
One had but to turn aside from the road at Warrener's

House, two miles beyond Morpeth, and thence proceed eastward for a further two, for ten castles to be seen at once from the vantage-point of Cockle Park Tower, itself a fine relic of a fortress belonging in the fifteenth century to the Ogles, situated now on a farm called by the hideous name of Blubberymires.

The peculiar appropriateness of Morpeth's name, meaning as it does " moor-path," is fully realised when coming up the road, up the well-named High Highlaws to where the road to Cockle Park Tower branches off, and where an old toll-house stands, with " Warrener's House," a deserted red-brick mansion, opposite. It is quite worth while to ask any passing countryman the name of that house, for then the " Northumbrian burr " will be heard in all its richness. As De Foe remarked, two hundred years ago, Northumbrians have " a Shibboleth upon their Tongues, namely, a difficulty in pronouncing the letter R," and in their mouths, consequently, the name becomes, grotesquely enough, " Wawwener."

Causey Park Bridge, over a little rivulet, a ruined windmill, and the remains of Causey Park Tower are the next features of the way before reaching a rise where an old road goes scaling a hillside to the right hand, surmounted by a farm picturesquely named " Helm-on-the-Hill." Thence downhill on to Bocken-field Moor, and then precipitously down again through West Thirston and across the picturesque bridge that spans the lovely Coquet, into Felton : villages bordering either bank of the river, where the angler finds excellent sport, and where the rash cyclist, regardless of the danger-boards erected for his guidance on the hill-tops, tries involuntary conclusions with the aforesaid bridge at the bottom. A mile onward, up the rising road, is the park of Swarland Hall, with " Nelson's Monument," a time-stained obelisk, seen amid the trees within the park fence, and showing against the sky-line as the traveller approaches the moorland height of Rushy Cap. Alexander Davison, squire of Swarland Hall and friend of the Admiral, erected it, " not to commemorate the

THE MARKET-PLACE, MORPETH.

public virtue and heroic achievements of Nelson, which is the duty of England, but to the memory of private friendship." Occupying so prominent a position by the roadside, it was probably intended to edify the coach-passengers of old. So to Newton-on-the-Moor—which might more fitly be named Newton-on-the-Hill—with its half a dozen cottages and its coal-pits, and thence by a featureless but not unpleasing road into Alnwick.

FELTON BRIDGE.

It is something of a shock to the sentimental pilgrim, northward-bound, that the entrance to historic Alnwick should be by the gas-works, the railway station, the Farmers' Folly (of which more shall presently be said), and other unmistakable and unromantic evidences of modernity that spread beyond the ancient confines of the town to form the suburb of Bondgate Without; but man cannot live by mediævalism alone. The town itself is gained at that point where the heavy blackened mass of Bondgate

itself spans the road, just beyond the elaborately
rebuilt " Old Plough," still exhibiting, however, the
curious tablet from the old house :—

That which your Father old hath purchased and left
You to possess, do you dearly
Hold to show his worthiness.   1714.

XXVII

ALNWICK is a town with a great past and a somnolent
present.   There are yawns at every turn, echoes with
every footfall, and grass growing unbidden in the
streets.   But there are forces of elemental power at
Alnwick, little though the stranger suspects them.
There have of late years been periods of storm and
stress in the columns of the *Alnwick Gazette*, for
instance, respecting the local water-supply, which
have drawn forth inappropriately fiery letters from
correspondents, together with many mixed metaphors.
How is this for impassioned writing ?—" The retribu-
tive forces of well-balanced justice have, after a dead
ebb, returned with a swelling tide, and overtaken the
arrogative policy of the freeholders."   But this is
nothing to the following striking figure of " the arm
of scandalous jobbery steeped to the lips in perfidious
dishonour ; " a delightful literary image unsurpassed in
Ireland itself ; or " another hydra of expense arising
phœnix-like from the ashes of misgovernment."   Did
the word " hydrant," we wonder, suggest this last
period ?   Is the dulness of Alnwick due to the decay
following the corruption hinted at ?   Perhaps, for,
as this publicist next inquires, " How could anything
symbolical of greatness, wrapped with ropes of sand,
ever and for aye, flourish like the green bay-tree ? "
Ah ! how ?   It is a difficult question to answer, and
so we will leave the question at that.
    Alnwick, of course, derives its name from its situation
on the romantic Aln : the " wick," or village on that

N

river. The name is kin to that of many other " wicks," " weeks," and " wykes " in England, and has its fellows in such places as High Wycombe ; Wykeham (now spelt Wickham) in Hampshire, whence came William of Wykeham ; the village of Weeke, near Winchester ; and in the town named simply Wick, in the north of Scotland. Alnwick in these times is a place of a certain grim and lowering picturesqueness. Its grey stone houses are at one with the greyness of the Northumbrian skies, and a general air of barren stoniness impresses the traveller as its chief feature. It is an effect of prisons and jailers which reaches its height in the open space that fronts the barbican of the castle. You look, instinctively, for His Majesty's prison regulations on the outer walls, and, approaching the gate, expect a warder's figure at the wicket.

This is no uncongenial aspect of that old fortress. It is rather in the Italian drawing-rooms, the picture-galleries, and the Renaissance luxuries of the interior of the castle that the jarring note is struck and all association with feudal times forgotten. Many a Border moss-trooper has unwillingly passed through this grim barbican, and so left the world for ever ; and many more of higher estate have found this old stronghold of the Percies a place of lifelong durance, or have in its dungeons met a secret end. For chivalry was not inconsistent with midnight murder or treachery, and the Percies, centred in their fortress like spiders in their webs, had all the virtues and the vices of chivalric times. Ambitious and powerful, they were alike a bulwark against the Scots and a menace to successive kings of England, and none in those olden times could have approached their castle gate with the equable pulsation of the modern tourist. In those times, instead of finding a broad level open space here, a deep ditch would have been seen and a drawbridge must have been lowered before access was possible. Then possibly the stone figures in violent attitudes that line the battlements, and seem to be casting missiles down upon the heads of visitors, may have been alarming ; to-day we only wonder if they could ever have tricked even the most bat-eyed warrior into a belief that they were really living men-at-arms.

The Percies, whose name attaches more than any other to Alnwick, were, strictly speaking, never its owners. The first of that name came over to England with the Conqueror in the person of William de Percy, a younger son of the feudal lord of the village of Percie in Normandy, which still exists to point out to the curious tourist the spot whence this historic family sprang. This William de Percy was nicknamed " Als Gernons," or " Whiskers," whence derives the name of Algernon, even now a favourite one with the Smithson-Percies. " Whiskers " was present at the battle of Hastings, and for his aid was granted manors in Hampshire, Lincolnshire, and York, but none in Northumberland. He died in 1086, when with the Crusaders, near Jerusalem. The Percies never became connected in any way with Alnwick, for the family of this William de Percy became extinct in 1166, when Agnes, an only child of his descendant, married Josceline de Lovaine ; and it was not until 1309 that the descendant of this Lovaine, who had assumed the Percy name, came into wrongful possession of the vast estates. Alnwick and sixty other baronies in Northumberland had until then been in possession of the de Vescis, of whom Yvo de Vesci was the original Norman owner. His descendant, William de Vesci, who died in 1297, was the last of his line, and appears to have been of a peculiarly trusting disposition. He put a great (and an unfounded) faith in the honesty of churchmen, leaving all his estates to Anthony Bek, Prince-Bishop of Durham, in trust for an infant illegitimate son, until he should come of age. But Bek picked a quarrel with his ward, and in 1309 sold the lands to Henry Percy, who thus became the first Baron Percy of Alnwick.

But let us not do an injustice to the Church. Prince-Bishops were kittle cattle, an amorphous kind of creature. Perhaps his lay half impelled Bek to this knavery, and, following the Scriptural injunction not to let the right hand know what is done by the left, his clerical moiety remained in ignorance of the crime. Heaven be praised, there are no longer any of these Jekyll and Hyde creatures, for the Bishops-Palatine of Durham were abolished two generations or more since.

There were, in the fulness of time, three Barons Percy of Alnwick, and then the Barony was erected into the Earldom of Northumberland. The axe and the sword took heavy toll of this new line, for the Earls of Northumberland seldom died in their beds, and father and son often followed one another in a bloody death, until at length they became extinct with the death of the eleventh and last Earl of Northumberland. Of these eleven, only seven died a natural death. There were Percies who fell in battle ; others who, rightly or wrongly, met the death of traitors ; one was torn to pieces by a mob ; and another was obscurely done to death in prison. Nor did only the heads of the family end violently ; their sons and other relations led lives as turbulent, and finished as suddenly.

The only child of the eleventh Earl of Northumberland was a daughter, Elizabeth Percy. She married firstly the Earl of Ogle ; secondly, Thomas Thynne of Longleat, who was murdered in Pall Mall in 1682 by Count Köningsmarck ; and thirdly, the sixth Duke of Somerset ; thus bringing the Percy estates into the Seymour family, and the Percy red hair as well.

It was of red-haired Elizabeth Percy, when Duchess of Somerset, that Dean Swift wrote the bitter and diabolically clever lines that are supposed to have lost him all chance of becoming a bishop. He wrote of her as " Carrots " :—

> Beware of carrots from Northumberland,
> Carrots sown *Thynne* a deep root may get,
> If so be they are in *Somer set ;*
> Their *cunnings mark* thou ; for I have been told
> They assassin when young and poison when old.
> Root out those carrots, O thou whose name
> Is backwards and forwards always the same

The one whose name was backwards and forwards alike

was Queen Anne, for Swift's purpose " Anna." It will be noticed that Swift not very obscurely hints that Elizabeth Percy connived at murder.

Her eldest son, the seventh Duke of Somerset, had, curiously enough, only one child, a daughter. She married " the handsomest man of his time," Sir Hugh Smithson, in 1740, and thus the property came into the hands of the present holders.

This most fortunate, as well as most handsome, fellow was Sir Hugh Smithson, one of a family of Yorkshire squires whose ancestor gained a baronetcy, created 1660, for his services to the Stuarts. Sir Hugh, born 1714, a son of Langdale Smithson, and grandson of another Sir Hugh, the third baronet, had little early prospect of much position in life. He was a younger son, and, like many another such, he went into trade. He was an apothecary. Having succeeded as fourth baronet to position and wealth, and with what he had made in commerce, the " handsomest man " made this very handsome marriage. He had the aristocratic instinct, and, discarding his old name, took that of Percy, to which, of course, he had no sort of right.

For him in 1749 was revived the old title, Earl of Northumberland, together with that of Baron Warkworth. In 1766 he became further, Duke of Northumberland and Earl Percy, and died 1786.

The name of Percy is one to conjure with. The Lovaines, who had assumed it, made it famous in the annals of chivalry, with a thousand deeds of derring-do in the debateable lands. Smithson, too, is a good name. It at least tells of descent from an honest craftsman, and Sir Hugh's knighted ancestor had, obviously, done nothing to be ashamed of. Unfortunately for Sir Hugh and his successors, this unwarranted assumption of an historic name took place so well within the historic period that it is never likely to be forgotten. George the Third, who also had the instinct of aristocracy, kept the fact well in mind, and when, sorely against his will, he was obliged to confer the Dukedom of Northumberland upon this ex-apothecary, consoled himself by vowing that he should never obtain the Order of the Garter. The duke personally solicited a blue ribbon from the king, and observed that he was " the first Percy who has been refused the Garter." " You forget," replied his Majesty, " that you are the first Smithson who has ever asked for it."

The huge and historic stronghold of Alnwick had by this time become ruinous, and the Smithson duke was for a while uncertain whether to reside here or at Warkworth. Alnwick, however, found favour with him, and he set to work to render it a place worthy of one of his quality. To this end he wrought havoc with the feudal antiquities of the castle, pulling down the ancient chapel and several of the towers, filling up the moats, plastering the walls and ceilings, enlarging arrow-slits into great windows, and playing the very devil with the place. The military history of the castle, as expressed in the picturesque irregularity of successive alterations and additions during many centuries, was swept away by his zeal for uniformity, and the interior rooms were remodelled in the taste of that age, to serve for a residence, to such an extent that only the outer walls retained even the appearance of a castle. When Pennant wrote of it in 1767, he said :—
" You look in vain for any marks of the grandeur of the feudal age ; for trophies won by a family eminent in our annals for military prowess and deeds of chivalry ; for halls hung with helms and hauberks " (good alliteration, that ! but rash for Cockney repetition), " or with the spoils of the chase ; for extensive forests or for venerable oaks. The apartments are large, and lately finished with a most incompatible elegance. The gardens are equally inconsistent, trim in the highest degree, and more adapted to a villa near London than to the ancient seat of a great baron." It was to this criticism of " trimness " that Bishop Percy objected. Discussing Pennant with Dr. Johnson, he could not sit quietly and hear him praise a man who had spoken so

disrespectfully of Alnwick Castle and the Duke's pleasure-grounds, and he eagerly opposed the Doctor, evidently with some heat, for Johnson said, " He has done what he intended ; he has made you very angry." To which the Bishop replied, " He has said the garden is trim, which is representing it like a citizen's parterre, when the truth is, there is a very large extent of fine turf and gravel walks."

" According to your own account, sir," rejoined Johnson, " Pennant is right. It *is* trim. Here is grass cut close and gravel rolled smooth. Is not that trim ? The extent is nothing against that ; a mile may be as trim as a square yard." The Bishop was vanquished.

All the sham Gothic alterations made at a huge outlay by the first Duke (with the exception of one room, which remains to show how atrocious his style was) were swept away by Algernon, the fourth Duke, about 1855, and at a still greater cost replaced internally with an interminable series of salons in the Italian style. Externally, the castle is a mediæval fortress ; internally it is an Italian palace. These works cost over £300,000, and serve to show the measure of ducal folly. Make a man a duke and give him an income commensurate, and he goes mad and builds and rebuilds, burying himself in masonry like a maggot in a cheese. But it is good for trade ; and perhaps that is why Providence allows a duke to be created now and then.

This magnificence for a long time created its own Nemesis, and the Dukes of Northumberland, in their gigantic castle, were worse off in one respect than a clerk in London suburbs in a six-roomed, nine-inch walled, jerry-built " villa " at £30 a year. They could never get a hot dinner ! The kitchen is large enough, and the fireplace so huge that the fire cannot be made up without shovelling on a ton of coals ; but the dining-room is so far away, and the communication was so bad (involving going across courtyards open to the sky) that everything was cold before it reached table. This has been remedied, and my lords dukes now have their food sent to them along rails on trolleys—just as they feed the beasts at the Zoo.

The Dukes of Northumberland are well titled. They are autocrats in that county, owning as they do 181,616 of its acres, and drawing a rental of £161,874. Some of them have been insufferably egotistical. The " Brislee " Tower, built on the neighbouring height of Brislaw by the first Duke, is evidence sufficient to prove that. It is a monument by himself to his own doings, and invites the pilgrim, in a long bombastical inscription, to " Look around, behold," and marvel at the plantations with which he caused the bare hillsides to be covered.

But the most prominent memorial in Alnwick is the well-named " Farmers' Folly," erected to the second Duke in 1816. Entering or leaving the town, it is a most striking object : a pillar 85 feet in height with the Percy lion on its summit. What did the second Duke do to deserve this ? Did he serve his country in war ? Was he a statesman ? Was he benevolent to the tenants who erected it ? Not at all. Here is the story.

When the nineteenth century dawned we were at war with France, and wheat and all kinds of produce were at enormously enhanced prices. The farmers, therefore, began to do very well. Their banking-accounts swelled, and some of them were on the way to realise small fortunes. The Duke saw this and sorrowed because they found it possible to do more than exist, and accordingly he added to their rents, doubling in almost every instance—and in many others quadrupling —them. But when the country entered on the long peace that followed Waterloo, and prices fell enormously, the unfortunate farmers found it impossible to pay their way under these added burdens. Mark the ducal generosity ! As they could not pay, he reduced the rents by twenty-five per cent. ! Like a draper at his annual sale, he effected a " great reduction," an " alarming sacrifice," by taking off a percentage of what he had already imposed. How

ALNWICK CASTLE FROM THE ROAD TO BELFORD.

noble! Then the tenants, the grateful fellows, subscribed to build the column, which is inscribed :— " To Hugh, Duke of Northumberland, by a grateful and united tenantry." Having done this, they went into bankruptcy and the workhouse, or emigrated, or just gave up their farms because they could not carry on any longer. The money they had subscribed did not suffice to complete this testimonial to Duke Hugh's benevolence, and so—a comic opera touch—he subscribed the rest, and finished it himself. What humorists these Smithsons are !

XXVIII

THE road, leaving Alnwick, plunges down from the castle barbican to the black hollow in which the Aln flows, overhung with interlacing and overarching trees. The river is crossed here by that bridge shown in Turner's picture, the " Lion Bridge " as it is called, from the Percy lion, " with tail stretched out as straight as a broom-handle," standing on the parapet and looking with steadfast gaze to the North. It is an addition since Turner's picture was painted, and an effective one, too. Also, since that time, the trees have encroached and enshrouded the scene most completely ; so that the only satisfactory view is that looking backwards when one has emerged from the black dell. And a most satisfactory view it is, with the i's and t's of romance dotted and crossed so emphatically that it looks like some theatrical scene, or the optically realised home of the wicked hero of one of Grimm's fairy tales. If this were not the beginning of the twentieth century, one might well think twice before venturing down into the inky depths of that over-shaded road ; but these are matter-of-fact times, and we know well that only the humdrum burgesses of Alnwick, in their shops, are beyond ; with, instead of a mediæval duke in the castle, who would think nothing of hanging a stray wayfarer or so from his battlements, only a very modern peer.

The road onwards is a weariness and an infliction to the cyclist, for it goes on in a heavy three miles' continuous rise up to the summit of Heiferlaw Bank, whence there is a wide and windy view of uncomfortable looking moorlands to the north, with the craggy Cheviots, perhaps covered with snow, to the north-west. As a literary lady—Mrs. Montagu—wrote in 1789, when on a northern journey, " These moors are not totally uninhabited, but they look unblest." How true !

The proper antidote to this is the looking back to where, deep down in the vale of Aln, lie town and castle, perhaps lapt in infrequent sunshine, more probably seen through rain, but, in any case, presenting a picture of sheltered content, and seeming to be protected from the rude buffets of the weather by the hill on which we are progressing and by the wooded flanks of Brislaw on the other side. " Seeming," because those who know Alnwick well could tell a different tale of wintry blasts and inclement seasons that belie the hint of this hillside prospect for three whole quarters round the calendar and a good proportion of the fourth. In this lies a suggestion of why the Percies were so warlike. They and their northern foes fought to keep themselves warm ! Nowadays such courses would lead to the police-court, and so football has become a highly-popular game in these latitudes. But the southward glimpse of Alnwick and its surroundings from the long rise of Heiferlaw Bank is, when sunshine prevails, of a quite incommunicable charm. The background of hills, covered with Duke Hugh's woods and crowned with his tower, recalls in its rich masses of verdure the landscapes of De Wint, and if in the Duke's inscription on that tower he seems to rank himself in fellowship with the Creator, certainly, now he has been dead and gone these hundred and twenty years, his saplings, grown into forest trees and clothing the formerly barren hillsides, have effected a wonderful change.

Beside the road are the few remaining stones of St. Leonard's Chapel, and, a short distance beyond, on the right, in a grove of trees, Malcolm's Cross, marking the spot where Malcolm Caenmore, king of Scotland,

MALCOLM'S CROSS.

was slain in 1093. It replaces a more ancient cross, and was erected by the first Duchess of Northumberland in 1774. It was on his seventh foray into Northumberland, besieging Alnwick Castle, that Malcolm was killed, in an ambush carefully prepared for him. The legend, which tells how he was treacherously slain by a thrust of a spear in the eye by one of the Percies, who was pretending to deliver up the castle keys on the spear's point, is untrue, as of course is the popular derivation of the family name from " pierce eye." Moreover, the Percies, as we have seen, did not own Alnwick until more than two hundred years afterwards.

Heiferlaw, as befits so commanding a hill-top so close to the Border, has its watch-tower, looking across the marches, whence the outlying defenders of Alnwick, ever watchful against Scottish raids, could give timely warning to the garrison.   It stands to-day a picturesque ruin, in cultivated fields that in those fierce old times, when men had no leisure for peaceful arts and industries, formed a portion of the wild moorland. " Blaw-weary," they call one of these fields, and the title is as descriptive of this exposed situation as anything in the whole range of nomenclature.   Beyond this point the road descends to a level stretch of country leading to North Charlton, where a few farmsteads alone stand for a village, together with a prominent hillock covered with trees and looking as though it had, or ought to have, a story to it ; a story which research fails to unearth.   Opposite, meadows called locally " Comby Fields," presumably from a series of ridges seen in them, seem to point to some forgotten history.   Brownyside, adjoining, is an expanse of moorland, covered with bracken, followed by Warenford, a pretty hamlet in a hollow by a tiny stream, with Twizel Park on the left.   At Belford, a large wide-streeted village with a nowadays all too roomy coaching inn, the " Blue Bell," and an old cross with gas-lamps fitted to it by some vandal or other, the road draws near the coast ; that storied Northumbrian sea-shore where Bambrough Castle on its islanded rock, many miles of yellow quicksands, and the Farne and Holy Islands are threaded out in succession before the gaze.   Bambrough, the apex of its pyramidical form, just glimpsed above an intervening headland, looks in the distance like another St. Michael's Mount, and Holy Island, ahead, is a miniature fellow to it.   The ruined cathedral of

Holy Island, the ancient Lindisfarne, the spot whence
the missionary Aidan from Iona began the conversion of
Northumbria in 634, and where he was succeeded by
that most famous of all northern bishops and saints, the
woman-hating St. Cuthbert, is the mother-church of the
north, and became possessed in later times of great
areas of land through which the road now passes.
Buckton, Goswick, Swinhoe, Fenwick, Cheswick, were
all " possessions " of the monastery ; and the old
ecclesiastical parish of Holy Island, once including all
these places on the mainland, and constituting then
an outlying wedge of Durham in the county of
Northumberland, although now a thing of the past,
still goes by the local name of Islandshire.   Buckton,
now a few scattered cottages by the roadside, held
a place in the old rhyme which incidentally shows that
the monks of Lindisfarne adopted that comforting
doctrine :

Who lives a good life is sure to live well.

Their farms and granges yielded them all that the
appreciative stomachs of these religious recluses could
desire, save indeed when the Scots swooped over the
Tweed and took their produce away.   It is a rhyme of
good living :—

From Goswick we've geese, from Cheswick we've cheese ;
From Buckton we've ven.son in store ;
From Swinhoe we've bacon, but the Scots it have taken,
And the Prior is longing for more.

The yellow sands that occupy the levels and reach
out at low tide to Holy Island are treacherous.   With
the exquisite colouring of sea and sky on a summer day
blending with them, they look at this distance like the
shores of fairyland ; but the grim little churchyard of
Holy Island has many memorials presenting another
picture—a picture of winter storm and shipwreck, for
which this wild coast has ever been memorable.
Off Bambrough, where the Farne Islands are scattered
in the sea, the scene is still recalled of the wreck of the
Forfarshire and Grace Darling's heroism ; and the

monument of that famous girl stands in Bambrough churchyard to render the summer pilgrim mindful of the danger of this coast. Dangerous not only to those on the waters, but also to travellers who formerly took the short cut from Berwick across the sands, instead of going by the hilly road. The way, clearly marked in daylight by a line of poles, has often been mistaken at night ; sudden storms, arising when travellers have reached midway, have swept them out to sea ; or fogs have entangled the footsteps even of those who knew the uncharted flats best. Whatever the cause, to be lost here was death. The classic instance, still narrated, is that of the postboy carrying the mails from Edinburgh on the 20th of November, 1725. Neither he nor the mail-bags was ever heard of again after leaving Berwick, and it was naturally concluded that he was lost on the quicksands in a sea-fog.

Away on the west of the road rise the Kyloe hills, like ramparts, and on their tallest ridge the church tower of Kyloe, conspicuous for long distances, and greatly appreciated by sailors as a landmark. The village is not perhaps famous, but certainly notable for a former vicar, who apparently aspired to writing a personal history of his parish as well as keeping a merely formal set of registers. Scattered through his official records are some very curious notes, among them : " 1696. Buried, Dec. 7, Henry, the son of Henry Watson of Fenwick, who lived to the age of 36 years, and was so great a fool that he could never put on his own close, nor never went a $\frac{1}{4}$ mile off ye house in all this space."

The road at this point was the scene of Grizel Cochrane's famous exploit, in 1685, when at night-fall, disguised as a man, and mounted on horseback, she waylaid the mail rider, and, holding a pistol to his head, robbed him of the warrant he was carrying for the execution of her father, Sir John Cochrane, taken in rebellion against James the Second. By this means she obtained a fortnight's respite, a delay which was used by his friends to secure his pardon.

Grizel Cochrane has, of course, been ever since the heroine of Border song. A clump of trees on a hillock, surrounded by a wall, to the right of the road, long bore the name of " Grizzy's Clump," but it has recently been felled and so much of the landmark destroyed. The country folk, possessed of the most invincible ignorance

BAMBROUGH CASTLE.

of the subject, know the place only as " Bambrough Hill," a title they have given it because from the summit an excellent view of Bambrough Castle is gained.

The plantations of Haggertson Castle now begin to cover the land sloping down toward the sea, and, after passing a deserted building on the left, once a coaching inn, the park surrounding the odd-looking modern castellated residence is reached. Here, by the entrance to the house, the road goes off at an acute angle to the left, and, continuing thus for a quarter of a mile, turns as sharply to the right. An old manorial pigeon-house, still with a vane bearing the initials C.L.H., stands by the way, and bears witness to the ownership of the estate in other times by the old Haggerston family. It was to Sir Carnaby Haggerston that those initials belonged, the late eighteenth-century squire who destroyed the old Border tower of Haggerston Castle, and built a new mansion in its stead, just as so many of his contemporaries did.

Sir Carnaby Haggerston does not appear—apart from this vandal act of his—to have been an especially Wicked Squire, although his devastating name launched him upon the world ear-marked for commission of all the crimes practised by the libertine landowners who made so brave a show in a certain class of literature and melodrama once popular. His name strikes the ear even more dramatically than that of Sir Rupert Murgatroyd, the accursed Baronet of Ruddigore in Mr. W. S. Gilbert's comic opera, but he never lived up to its possibilities. The only things he seems to have had in common with the typical squire of old seem to have been a love of port and whist, and a passion for building houses too large for his needs or means.

The Wicked Squire who unwillingly sat to the novelists who used to write in the pages of *Reynolds' Miscellany* and journals of that stamp fifty years ago, as the high-born villain of their gory romances, may be regretted, because without him the pages of the penny novelist are become extremely tame ; but his disappearance need not be mourned for any other reasons.

It is to him we owe the many supposedly " classical " mansions that, huge and shapeless, like so many factories, reformatories, or workhouses, affront the green sward, the beautiful gardens, and the noble trees of many English parks. To build vast mansions of this " palatial " character, the squires often pulled down middle-Tudor or Elizabethan, or even earlier manor-houses of exquisite beauty, vying with one another in the size and extravagance of the new buildings, whose original cost and subsequent maintenance have during the past hundred and fifty years kept many county families in straitened circumstances, and do so still. There was a squire who pulled down a

o

whole series of mediæval wayside crosses in his district,
and used the materials as building-stones toward the
great mansion he was erecting for the purpose of
outshining a neighbour. Those transcendent squires,
the noblemen of old, had larger opportunities and made
the worst use of them. The Duke of Buckingham,
for example, bought a property, demolished the
Elizabethan hall that stood on it, and built Stowe there
in its place ; a building of vast range and classic
elevation with colonnades and porticoes, and " windows
that exclude the light and lead to nothing," as some one
has very happily remarked. Sir Francis Dashwood,
that hero of the Hell Fire Club, pulled down West
Wycombe church and built the existing building, that
looks like a Lancashire cotton-mill, and every one built
houses a great deal larger than were wanted or they
could afford ; which, like the Earl of Leicester's seat at
Holkham were so little like homes that they could
neither live in their stately apartments nor sleep in
their vast bedrooms. Like the Earl and Countess of
Leicester, who were compelled for comfort's sake to
sleep in one of the servants' bedrooms in the attics,
they lived as settlers in corners of their cavernous
and uncomfortable palaces.

Pity the poor descendant of the Squires ! He
cannot afford in these days to keep up his huge house ;
to pull it down would in itself cost a fortune ; and its
very size frightens the clients of the house-agent in
whose hands he has had it for letting, these years past.
All over England this is seen, and the old Yorkshire
tale would stand true of any other county and of many
other county magnates of that time. The Marquis of
Rockingham, according to that story, built a mansion
at Wentworth big enough for the Prince of Wales ;
Sir Rowland Winn built one at Nostel Priory fit for the
Marquis of Rockingham ; and Mr. Wrightson of
Cusworth built a house fit for Sir Rowland Winn.
No doubt the farmers carried on the tale of extrava-
gance down to their stratum of society, and so *ad
infinitum*.

But to return to Haggerston Castle, which now belongs to the Leylands. Conspicuous for some distance is the tower built of recent years to at one and the same time resemble a mediæval keep and to serve a practical purpose as a water-tower, engine-room, and look-out. The place, however, is remarkable for quite other things than its mock castle, for in the beautiful park are kept in pens, or roaming about freely, herds of foreign animals which make of it a miniature Zoological Gardens. It is, in a sense, superior indeed to that well-known place, for if the collections do not cover so wide a range, the animals are in a state of nature. Emus, Indian cattle, kangaroos, and many varieties of wild buck roam this " paradise," together with a thriving herd of American bison. The bison is almost extinct, even in his native country, but here he flourishes exceedingly and perpetuates his kind. A bison bull is a startling object, come upon unawares, and looks like the production of a lunatic artist chosen to illustrate, say, the Jabberwock in *Alice in Wonderland*. He is all out of drawing, with huge shaggy forelegs, and head and shoulders a size too large for the rest of his body; an eye like a live coal, tufted coat, like a worn-out door-mat, and uncomfortable-looking horns : the kind of creature that inhabits Nightmare Country, popularly supposed to be bred of indigestion and lobster mayonnaise.

XXIX

BEYOND Haggerston, and up along the rising road that leads for six of the seven miles to Berwick, the journey is unexpectedly commonplace. The road has by this time turned away from the sea, and when it has led us through an entirely charming tunnel-like avenue of dwarf oaks, ceases to be interesting. Always upwards, it passes collieries, the " Cat " inn, and the hamlet of Richardson's Stead or Scremerston, whence, arrived at the summit of Scremerston Hill, the way down into Tweedmouth and across the Tweed into Berwick is clear.

Tweedmouth sits upon the hither shore of Tweed, clad in grime and clinkers. Like a mudlark dabbling in the water but not cleansing himself in it, Tweed-mouth seems to acquire no inconsiderable portion of its dirt from its foreshore. Engineering works and coal-shoots are responsible for the rest. Little or nothing of antiquity enlivens its mean street that leads down to the old bridge and so across the Tweed into Scotland. The roofs of Berwick, clustered close together and scaling one over the other as the town ascends the opposite shore of the river, are seen, with the spired Town Hall dominating all at the further end of the long, narrow, hump-backed old structure, and away to the left that fine viaduct of the North Eastern Railway, the Royal Border Bridge. But the finest view, and the most educational in local topo-graphy, is that gained by exploring the southern shore of the Tweed for half a mile in an easterly direction. An unlovely waterside road, it is true, a maze of railway arches spanning it, and shabby houses hiding all but the merest glimpses of Tweed-mouth church and its gilded salmon vane, referring to the salmon-fishery of the Tweed, but leading to a point of view whence the outlook to the north-west is really grand. There, across the broad estuary of the Tweed, lies Berwick, behind its quays and its enclosing defences. Across the river, in the middle distance, goes Berwick Bridge, its massive piers and arches looking as though carved out of the rock, rather than built up of single stones. Beyond it, in majestic array, go the tall arches of the Royal Border Bridge, and, in the background, are the Scottish hills. Tweedmouth, its timber jetty, its docks, and church spire, and its waterside lumber are in the forefront. This, then, is the situation of Berwick, for centuries the best-picked bone of contention between the rival countries of England and Scotland; the Border

THE SCOTTISH BORDER: BERWICK TOWN AND BRIDGE FROM TWEEDMOUTH.

cockpit, geographically in the northern kingdom, but
wrested from it by the masterful English seven hundred
and fifty years ago, and taken and re-taken by or from
stubborn Scots on a round dozen of occasions afterwards. Sieges, assaults, stormings, massacres under
every condition of atrocity ; these are the merest
commonplaces of Berwick's story, until the mid-
sixteenth century ; and the historian who would write
of its more unusual aspects must needs turn attention
to the rare and short-lived interludes of peace.

It was in 1550, during the short reign of Edward
the Sixth, that the existing fortifications enclosing the
town were begun, whose river-fronting walls are so
conspicuous from Tweedmouth. The old bridge, built
by James the First, was the first peaceful enterprise
between the two kingdoms, for, although Berwick had
for over a century been recognised as a neutral or
" buffer " state, peace went armed for fear of accidents,
and easy communication across the Tweed was not
encouraged. There is food for reflection in comparison
between that bridge and the infinitely greater work of
the railway viaduct. The first, 1,164 feet in length,
with only 17 feet breadth between the parapets,
bridging the river with fifteen arches, cost £17,000,
and took twenty-four years to build ; the railway
bridge of twenty-eight giant arches, each of $61\frac{1}{2}$ feet
span, and straddling the Tweed at a height of 129 feet,
was built in three years, at a cost of £120,000. The
" Royal Border Bridge," as it was christened at its
opening by the Queen, has precisely the appearance
of a Roman aqueduct and belongs to the Stone and
Brick Age of railways. Were it to do over again,
there can be no doubt that, instead of a long array of
graceful arches, half a dozen lengths of steel lattice
girders would span the tide. It was at a huge cost
that England and Scotland were thus joined by rail ;
bridge and approaches swallowing up the sum of
£253,000. The first passenger train crossed over,
October 15, 1848, but the works were not finally
completed until 1850. In the August of that year the

Queen formally opened it, nearly two years after it was
actually opened ; a fine object-lesson for satirists.
How we laugh at ceremonials less absurd than this
when they take place in China and Japan.

Berwick town is seen, on entering its streets, to
be unexpectedly modern and matter-of-fact. The
classically steepled building that bulks commandingly
in the main thoroughfare and looks like a church is the
Town Hall, and displays the arms of Berwick prominently, the municipal escutcheon supported on either
side by a sculptured bear sitting on his rump and
surrounded by trees. It is thus that one of the
disputed derivations of Berwick's name is alluded to.
At few towns has the origin of a place-name been so
contested as at Berwick ; and, for all the pother about
it, the question is still, and must remain, unanswered.
It might as reasonably have come from *aberwic*, the
mouth of a river, as from *bergwic*, the hillside village,
and much more reasonably than from the fanciful
" bar " prefix alluding to the bareness of the country ;
while of course the legend that gives the lie to that last
variant, and seeks an origin in imaginary bears
populating mythical woods, is merely infantile.

The church-like Town Hall, which is also a market-
house and the town gaol, does indeed perform one of
the functions of a church, for the ugly Puritan parish
church of the town has no tower, and so the steeple of
the Town Hall rings for it.

In the broad High Street running northward from
this commanding building are all the prominent inns
of the town, to and from which the coaches came
and went until the opening of the Edinburgh and
Berwick Railway in 1846. Some of the short stages
appear to have been misery-boxes, according to Dean
Ramsay, who used to tell an amusing anecdote of
one of them. On one occasion a fellow-traveller at
Berwick complained of the rivulets of rain-water
falling down his neck from the cracked roof. He
drew the coachman's attention to it on the first
opportunity, but all the answer he got was the matter-

of-fact remark, " Ay, mony a ane has complained
o' *that* hole."

The mail-coaches leaving Berwick on their journey
north were allowed to take an extra—a fourth—outside
passenger. Mail-coaches running in England were,
until 1834, strictly limited to four inside and three
outside. Of these last, one sat on the box, beside the
coachman, while the other two were seated immediately
behind, on the fore part of the roof, with their backs
to the guard. This was a rule originally very strictly
enforced, and had its origin in the fear that, if more
were allowed, it would be an easy matter for
desperadoes to occupy the seats as passengers and to
suddenly overpower both coachman and guard. The
guard in his solitary perch at the back, with his sword-
case and blunderbuss ready to hand, could have shot
or slashed at those in front, on his observing any
suspicious movement, and it is somewhat surprising
that no nervous guard ever did wound some innocent
passenger who may have turned round to ask him a
question. The concession of an extra seat on the
outside of coaches entering Scotland was granted to
the mail-contractors in view of the more widely
scattered population of Scotland, and of the comparative scarcity of chance passengers on the way.

But there is very great uncertainty as to the number
of passengers allowed on the mails in later years.
Moses Nobbs, one of the last of the old mail-guards,
states that no fewer than eight passengers were
allowed outside at the end of the coaching age.
Doubtless this was owing both to the complaints of
the contractors that with the smaller complement they
could not make the business pay, and to the growing
security of the roads.

Royal proclamations used, until recent times, to
specifically mention " our town of Berwick-upon-
Tweed " when promulgating decrees, for as by treaty
an independent State, neither in England nor Scotland,
laws and ordinances affecting Great Britain and
Ireland could not legally be said to have been extended

to Berwick without the especial mention of " our town." A state whose boundaries north and south were Lamberton Toll and the Tweed, a distance of not more than four miles, with a corresponding extent from east to west, it was thus on a par with many a petty German principality. Nearly three-quarters of the land comprised within " Berwick Bounds " is the property of the Corporation, having been granted by James the First when, overjoyed at his good fortune in succeeding to the English crown and thus uniting those of the two countries, he entered upon his heritage. Lucky Berwick ! Its freehold property brings in a revenue of £18,000 a year, in relief of rates.

If the streets of Berwick are disappointing in so historic a place, then let the pilgrim make the circuit of the town on the ramparts. These, at least, tell of martial times, as also do the fragmentary towers of the old castle, the few poor relics left of that stronghold by the modern railway station overhanging a deep cleft. Then, away in advance of the ramparts, still thrusting its tubby, telescopic, three-storied form forward, is the old Bell Tower, where, in this advanced post, the vigilant garrison kept eyes upon the north, whence sudden Scottish raids might be developed at any time.

Grass covers the ramparts and sprouts in tufts upon the gun-platforms contrived in early Victorian days upon them, and almost every variety of obsolete cannon, short of the demi-culverins with which Drake searched the Spanish Main, go to make up what—Heaven help them and us !—War Office officials call batteries. Guns bristle thickly upon the waterside batteries overlooking the harbour, but not one of them is modern. All are muzzle-loading pieces, fit for an artillerist's museum, and their carriages—where they are mounted at all—are in bewildering variety, principally, however, of rotting wood. The most recent piece, an Armstrong gun not less than fifty years old, lies derelict in the long grass, and children amuse themselves by filling its hungry-looking maw with clods. Pot-bellied like all the old Armstrongs, it has a look as though it had grown fat and lazy with that diet and lain down in the long grass to sleep. Perhaps to guard its slumbers, a War Office notice beside the prostrate gun vainly forbids trespassing !

Down in a ditch of the fortifications a soldier in his shirt sleeves, his braces dangling about his legs, is tending early peas with all the tenderness of a mother for an invalid child ; for, look you, early peas in these latitudes have a hard fight for it ; and the fight of those vegetables for existence against the nipping blasts that sweep from off the North Sea is the only sign of warfare the place has to show. Taken as a whole, and looked at whichever way you will, the " defences " of Berwick-upon-Tweed show a trustfulness in Providence and in the astounding luck of the British Empire which argues much for the piety or the folly of our rulers. And so, with the varied reflections these things call forth, let us away up the High Street, and, passing under the archway of the Scotch Gate, spanning its northern extremity, leave Berwick on the way to Scotland.

XXX

" Seeing Scotland, Madam," said Dr. Johnson, in answer to Mrs. Thrale's expressed wish to visit that country, " is only seeing a worse England. It is seeing the flower gradually fade away to the naked stalk." This bitter saying of the Doctor's comes vividly to mind when leaving Berwick on the way to Edinburgh. Passing the outskirts of the town at a point marked on the Ordnance map with the unexplained name of " Conundrum," the country grows bare and treeless on approaching the sea, and at Lamberton Toll, three miles north, where " Berwick Bounds " are reached and Scotland entered, the scene is desolate in the extreme. The cottage to the left of the road at this point, formerly the toll-house of the turnpike-gate that stood here, is a famous place, rivalling Gretna Green for the runaway matches, legalised at the gate until 1856, when changes in the law rendered a part of the once-familiar notice in the window out-of-date. It ran, " Ginger-beer sold here, and marriages performed on the most reasonable terms " ; an announcement which for combination of the trivial and the tremendous it would be difficult to beat.

Geographically in Scotland when across the Tweed, we are not politically in that country until past this

LAMBERTON TOLL.

cottage. Then indeed we are, in many ways, in a foreign country.

Scots law is a fearful and wonderful variant from English. Even its terminology is strange to the English ear, which finds—hey, presto !—on passing Berwick Bounds, a barrister changed into an " advocate," a solicitor converted into a " Writer to the Signet," and a prosecutor masquerading under the thrilling and descriptive alias of " pursuer." It was the laxity of Scots law that made, not only Gretna Green, but any other place over the Border from England, a resort of those about to marry and impatient of constraints, legal or family, at any period between 1753 and 1856. Gretna Green and its neighbour, Springfield, in especial, and in no small degree Lamberton Toll, were the scenes of much hasty marrying during that space of time. Marrying, *bien entendu*, and not giving in marriage, for

these were runaway matches, and those whose position
it was to give, and who withheld their consent,
generally came posting up to the toll-gate in pursuit
just in time to hear the last words of the simple but
effective ritual of the toll-keeper who had witnessed the
declaration of the truants that, " This is my wife," and
" This is my husband," a simple form of words which,
uttered in the presence of a witness, was all that the
beneficent legal system of Scotland required as marriage
ceremony.   This form completed, and for satisfaction's
sake a rough register subscribed, the indignant parent,
who possibly had been battering on the outside of the
door, was admitted and introduced to his son-in-law.

It was a century of licence (not marriage licence), that
prevailed on the Border from the passing of Lord
Hardwicke's Clandestine Marriage Act in 1753 until
that of Lord Brougham in 1856, which put a stop to
this " over the Border " marrying by rendering
unions illegal on the part of those not domiciled in
Scotland, which had not been preceded by a residence
in that kingdom of not less than twenty-one days by
one or other of the contracting parties.

There was no special virtue in the first place across
the Border-line at any point, nor did it matter who
" officiated," the person who " performed the ceremony " being only a witness and in no sense a
clergyman ; but it was obviously, with these legal
facilities, the prime object of runaway couples pressed
for time, and with hurrying parents and guardians
after them, to seize their opportunity at the first place,
and at the hands of the first person in that liberal
minded land.   Not that the Kirk looked benevolently
upon this.   It fined them, for discipline's sake, and the
happy couples cheerfully paid, for by doing so they
acquired the last touch of validity, which, on the face
of it, could not be called into dispute.   ·

One of this long line of Hymen's secular priesthood
at Lamberton Toll had, early in the nineteenth century,
an unhappy time of it, owing to an error of judgment
and an ignorance of the law scarcely credible.   Joseph

OFF TO THE BORDER.

Atkinson, the toll-keeper, was away one day at
Berwick when a runaway pair arrived at the gate.
His wife, or another, sent them after him, and in
Berwick the ceremony, such as it was, was performed.
Now Berwick is a county of itself, and the inhabitants
boast, or used to, that their town belongs to neither
England nor Scotland. It is hinted (by those who do
not belong to Berwick) that it belongs instead to the
devil, which possibly is a reminiscence of the townsfolk's
smuggling days, on the part of those who duly render
unto Cæsar. This by the way. Unhappily for
Mr. Joseph Atkinson, Berwick owes allegiance to
English law, as he found when his ceremony was
declared null and void, and he was duly sentenced to
seven years transportation for having contravened the
Marriage Act of 1753.

Halidon Hill, where the English avenged Bannockburn upon the Scots in 1333, is on the crest of the
upland to the west of Lamberton Toll. Now the road
runs upon the edge of the black cliffs that plunge down
into the North Sea, commanding bold views of a stern
and iron-bound coast. Horses, coachmen, guards, and
passengers alike quailed before the storms that swept
these exposed miles, and even the highwaymen sought
other and more sheltered spots. Macready, on tour
in the north, was snowed up here, in the severe winter
of 1813-14. Coming south through the deep and still
falling snow, he travelled in a cutting made in the drifts
for miles between Ross Inn and Berwick-on-Tweed.
" We did not reach Newcastle," he says, " until nearly
two hours after midnight : and fortunate was it for the
theatre and ourselves that we had not delayed our
journey, for the next day the mails were stopped ; nor
for more than six weeks was there any conveyance by
carriage between Edinburgh and Newcastle. After
some weeks, a passage was cut through the snow for
the guards to carry the mails on horseback, but for a
length of time the communications every way were very
irregular."

Where the little Flemington Inn stands solitary at

a fork of the road, close by a tremendous gap in the cliffs, is placed Burnmouth station, on the main line, wedged in a scanty foothold, hundreds of feet above the sea. Day or night it is a picturesque place, but more especially in the afterglow of sunset, when the inky blackness of the rift in the cliffs can still be set off against the gleam of the sea, caught in a notch of the rocks, and when the lighted signal-lamps of the little junction glow redly against the sky on their tall masts, like demon eyes. A fishlike, if not an ancient, smell lingers here, for Burnmouth station is constantly in receipt of the catches made down below by the hardy fishers of the three hamlets of Burnmouth, Partinghal, and Ross, queer fishing villages of white-washed stone cottages that line the rocky shore unsuspected by ninety-nine among every hundred travellers along the road above. Herrings caught in the North Sea are cured here, packed in barrels, and sent by rail to distant markets.

Ayton, two miles onward, away from the sea, is entered in perplexing fashion, downhill and by a sharp turn to the right over a bridge spanning the Eye Water, instead of continuing straight ahead along a road that makes spacious pretence of being the proper way. Ayton itself, beyond being a large village, with a modern castellated residence in the Scottish baronial style and vivid red sandstone at its entrance, is not remarkable.

Leaving Ayton, the road enters a secluded valley whose solitudes of woodland, water, and meadows are not imperilled, but only intensified, by the railway, which goes unobtrusively within hail of this old coaching highway. On the right rise the gently swelling sides of a range of hills sloping upwards from the very margin of the road and covered with woods of dwarf oak, through whose branches the sunlight filters and lies on the ferns below in twinkling patches of gold. Here stood the old Houndwood Inn, and the building yet remains, converted—good word in such a connection—into a manse for the Free Church near by, itself a building calculated to make angels weep ; if angels have appreciations in architecture. Another, and a humbler, building carries on the licensed victualling trade, and calls itself, prettily enough, the " Greenwood Inn." It is, in fact, a stretch of country that makes for inspiration in the rustic sort. If there were a sign of the " Robin Hood " here we should acclaim it romantic and appropriate, even though tradition tells not of that mythical outlaw in these marches. If not Robin, then some other chivalric outlaw surely should have pervaded the glades of Houndwood, open as they are, with never a fence, a hedge, or a ditch to the road, just as though these were still the fine free days of old, before barbed-wire fences were dreamed of, or notices to trespassers set up, threatening vague penalties to be enforced " with all the rigour of the law," as the phrase generally runs.

It is a valley of whose delights one must needs chatter, although with but dim hopes of communicating much of its charm. Through it that little stream called by the medicinally sounding name, the Eye Water, wanders with a feminine hesitancy and inconstancy of purpose. It flows all ways by turns and never long in any direction, and with so many amazing loops and doublings, that it might well defy the precision of the Ordnance chartographers themselves. We bid farewell to this fickle stream at Grant's House, and scrape acquaintance with another, the Pease Burn, flowing in another direction. For Grant's House stands on the watershed which orders the going of several watercourses. It is also the summit level of this railway route to the North. Here, quite close to the road, is Grant's House station, and here, bordering the road itself, are the houses that form Grant's House itself. This sounds like speaking in paradox, but the place is a village, or rather a scattered collection of pretty cottages that have gathered around the one inn which was the home of the original Grant. The place-name seems to hint of other and less-travelled times, when these Borders were sparsely settled and wayfarers few ; when but one house served to take the edge off the solitude, and that an inn kept by one Grant. The imagination, thus uninstructed, weaves cocoons of speculation around these premises and conceives him to have been a host of abounding personality, thus to hand his name down to posterity, preserved in a place-name, like a fly in amber. But all speculations that start upon this innkeeping basis would be incorrect, for this sponsorial Grant was the contractor who made the road from Berwick to Edinburgh, building a cottage for himself in this then lonely spot, which only in later years became the Grant's House inn.

More streams and woods beyond this point, and then comes the long and toilsome rise up to Cockburnspath, past Pease Burn, where the road takes a double *S* curve on the hillside, and other tall hills, to right and left and ahead, largely covered with firs and larches, seem to look on with a gloomy anticipation of some one, less cautious than his fellows, breaking his neck. Where there are no hillside woods there are grass meadows in which, if it be June or July, the haymakers can be seen from the road, haymaking, with attendant horses and carts, at a perilous angle. The Pease Burn, flowing deep down in its Dene, is spanned at a height of 127 feet, half a mile down stream, by a four-arched bridge, built in 1786.

XXXI

SET in midst of these steep and twisting roads and above these watery ravines is Cockburnspath Tower, a ruined Border castle of rust-red stone that frowns down upon the road on the edge of a tremendous gully. It was never more than a peel-tower, but strongly placed and solidly built, a fitting refuge for those who took part in the ups and downs of Border forays. In the days when Co'path Tower (local pronunciation) was built, every one's house was more or less a defensible building. "An Englishman's house is his castle" is a figurative expression commonly used to prefigure the inviolate character of the law-abiding citizen's domicile, but it might have been said literally of dwellers in these debateable lands. The more property he possessed, the stronger was the Border farmer's tower. When the moss-troopers and mediæval scoundrels of every description were on the warpath, or merely out on a cattle-lifting expedition, these embattled agriculturists shut themselves up in their safe retreats. The lower floor, on a level with the ground, received the live stock ; the floor above, the servants ; and to the topmost story, as the safest situation, the family retired. The gate below was of iron, for your Border reiver was no squeamish sort, and would burn these domestic garrisons alive without hesitation. Therefore in the most approved type of fortress there was nothing inflammable. Sympathy, however, would be wasted on those old-time cultivators, for they all took a turn at armed cattle-lifting as occasion offered, and found the readiest way of stocking their farms with every requisite to be that of stealing what they required.

> For why ? Because the good old rule
> Sufficeth them : the simple plan
> That they should take who have the power,
> And they should keep who can.

Short and sudden forays were characteristic of this kind of life. The Border cattle-lifter came and went in the twinkling of an eye, and drove the captured flocks and herds away with him at a rate no merely honest drover ever marshalled his sheep and heifers to market. There must have been many highly desirable, but inanimate and not easily portable, things which the raiders were obliged to leave behind, as one of this kidney regretted in casting a last glance at a hayrick he had no means of lifting. "Had ye but four feet, ye suld no stand lang there," said he, as he turned to go.

The mouldering old tower here at Cockburnspath belonged to the Earls of Home. Beautifully situated for preying upon occasional travellers, the glen and the foaming torrent below have no doubt received the bodies of many a one who in the old days was rash enough to pass within sight of the old tower. The comparatively modern bridge that takes a flying leap across the ravine is the successor of an ancient one of narrower span that still, covered with moss and ferns, arches over the water, deep down in the hollow, and is popularly supposed to be the oldest bridge in Scotland. A dense tangle of red-berried rowan-trees, firs, and oaks overhangs the gorge. Altogether a place that calls insistently to be sketched and painted, but a place, from the military point of view, to be wary of ; being a position, as Cromwell in one of his despatches says, " where one man to hinder is better than twelve to make way." It was at the " strait pass at Copperspath," as he calls it, that the great general, writing after the battle of Dunbar, found plenty to hinder.

If ever general profited more by the mistakes of the enemy than by his own tactical ability, it was Cromwell at this juncture. The Scots under Leslie had cooped him up at Dunbar, and, surrounded by the enemy, who occupied the heights and closed every defile that led to a possible line of retreat, he must, diseased and famishing as were his forces, have capitulated, for the sea was at his back, and no help possible from that direction. It was then that Leslie made his disastrous move from the hills, and came down upon the English in the levels of Broxburn, to the south of Dunbar town, where Cromwell had his headquarters ; and it was then that Cromwell, seizing the moment when the enemy, coming down in a dense mass upon a circumscribed space by Broxburn Glen, retrieved the situation, and, directing a cavalry movement upon Leslie's forces, had the supreme relief of seeing them broken up and stamped into the earth by the furious charge of his horsemen. The fragments of the Scottish army, routed with a slaughter of three thousand, and ten thousand prisoners, fled, and Cromwell's contemplated retreat to Berwick was no longer a necessity. Indeed, the

COCKBURNSPATH TOWER.

whole of the Lowlands of Scotland now lay open before him, and he entered Edinburgh with little opposition.

It is a distance of nine miles between the village of Cockburnspath and Dunbar, the road going parallel with the sea all the way. First it goes dizzily over the profound rift of Dunglass Dene, spanned at a height of a hundred and twenty-five feet above the rocky bed of a mountain stream by the bold arch of the railway viaduct and by the road bridge itself. It is a scene of rare beauty, and the walk by the zigzagging path among the thickets and the trees, down to where the sea comes pounding furiously into a little cove, a quarter of a mile below, wholly charming. Away out to sea is the lowering bulk of the Bass Rock, a constant companion in the view approaching Dunbar.

The direct road for Edinburgh avoids Dunbar altogether, forking to the left at Broxburn where the battlefield lay, where the burn still flows across the road as it did on the day of " Dunbar Drove," as Carlyle calls that dreadful rout. Here " the great road then as now crosses the Burn of Brock.
Yes, my travelling friends, vehiculating in gigs or otherwise over that piece of London road, you may say to yourselves, Here, without monument, is the grave of a valiant thing which was done under the Sun ; the footprint of a Hero, not yet quite undistinguishable, is here ! "
Ahead, with its great red church on a hillock, still somewhat apart of the south end of the town, is Dunbar, the first characteristically Scottish place to which we come. It is not possible to compete with Carlyle's masterly word-picture of it, which presents the place before you with so marvellous a fidelity to its spirit and appearance :—" The small town of Dunbar stands high and windy, looking down over its herring-boats, over its grim old castle, now much honeycombed, on one of those projecting rock-promontories with which that shore of the Firth of Forth is niched and vandyked as far as the eye can reach. A beautiful sea ; good land too, now that the plougher understands his trade ;

a grim niched barrier of whinstone sheltering it from the chafings and tumblings of the big blue German Ocean." There you have Dunbar.

Let us add some few details to the master's fine broad handling; such as the fact that its streets are

THE TOLBOOTH, DUNBAR.

wondrously cobble-stoned, that those whinstone rocks are red and give a dull, blood-like coloration to the scene, and that the curious old whitewashed Tolbooth in the High Street is the fullest exemplar of the Scottish architectural style. Windy it is, as Carlyle says, and with a rawness in its air that calls forth shivers from the Southron even in midsummer. Here the stranger new to Scotland is apt to see for the first time the sturdy fishwives and lasses who, still often with bare feet, go along the streets carrying prodigiously weighty baskets of fish on their backs, sometimes secured by a leather strap that goes from the basket around the head and forehead !

One leaves Dunbar by wriggly and exiguous streets, coming through the fisher villages of Belhaven and West Barns to where the main avoiding route rejoins at Beltonford. The Scottish Tyne winds through the flat meadows on the right—at such fortunate times, that is to say, as when it does not pretend to be an inland sea and take the meadows, the road, and the railway for its province. The road, too, is flat, and the railway, which hugs it closely, the same. A good road, too, and beautiful. Midway of it, towards East Linton, are the farmsteads and ricks of Phantassie, at which spot Rennie, the engineer who built London Bridge, and heaven and Dr. Smiles alone know how many harbours, was born in 1761. " Phantassie " is a name that sorely piques one's curiosity, so odd is it ; but the group of farm-buildings is commonplace enough, if more than commonly substantial. No fantasy in their design, at any rate.

At East Linton we cross the Tyne which, crawling through the meadows, plunges here in cascades under the road bridge, amid confused rocks. The railway crosses it too, close by, and spans the road beyond ; and the village huddles together at an angle of the way. A long ascent out of it commands wide views of agricultural Haddingtonshire, and of that surprising mountainous hill, Traprain Law, rising out of the plain to a height of over seven hundred feet.

Not merely a surprising hill, but one with an astonishing story. It had always been thought that treasure was buried there, among the traces of ancient buildings ; and accordingly, with the the permission of Right Honourable A. J. Balfour, on whose land the hill is situated, excavations were begun in 1919. It was found that the hill-top had been inhabited intermittently over remote periods, and diggings were made into successive strata of hearths and floorings. At first the " finds " were of minor articles : bronze ornaments, glass and pottery, fragments of iron, mostly of Celtic origin, but some Roman. The great discovery was made on May 12th, 1919, when a workman, driving a pick through a floor, brought up a silver bowl on the point of it. A deep recess was then discovered, filled with treasure : bowls, spoons, cups, saucers, and a miscellaneous collection of plate, mostly cut to pieces in strips folded over and hammered down into packets of silver. Although it was grievous to look upon that destruction, a good many of the fragments retained their original decoration. They appear to be partly of Romano-Christian origin, for the sacred symbol occurs among them, and on one piece is the inscription " Jesus Christus." Other pieces are almost as certainly pagan, bearing as they do figures of Pan and Hercules. Among them were four coins : the earliest of the Emperor Valerius, whose reign began A.D. 364, and the latest of Honorius, who died A.D. 463. A metal belt of Saxon character was among this treasure-trove.

It appeared, therefore, that this hoard was a relic of one of the sea-rovers' raids on this coast in the fifth or sixth century, and that the spoils had in some cases come from plundered religious houses. The raiders were perhaps disturbed in their activities, and buried their loot in the expectation of returning for it at some more suitable time.

But they never returned. What happened to them is a vain conjecture. They may have been found here and slain by some stronger force, and perhaps they were lost at sea. In any case, their hoard lay here for close upon one thousand five hundred years. What they had hoped to carry away is now an exhibit in the Scottish National Museum at Edinburgh.

To the north-going cyclist the road presently makes ample amends for the mile-long rise, for, once topping it, a gentle but continuous descent of four miles leads into Haddington, down a road that for the most part could scarce be bettered, so excellent its surface, so straight its course, and so beautifully sylvan its surroundings. Hailes Castle is finely seen on the left during this descent, its ruined walls and ivy-covered towers wrapped three parts round with the thick woodlands that clothe the lower slopes of Traprain Law. Mary, Queen of Scots, and her evil spirit, the sinister Bothwell, had Hailes Castle for their bower of love, and Wishart the martyr had a cell in it for a prison, so that its present beauty of decay lacks nothing of historic interest.

Nor does the fine mansion of Amisfield, through whose park-like lands the road now descends. Amisfield has lurid associations. Under the name of New Mills, it was in 1687 the scene of a dreadful parricide, and was at a later period purchased by the infamous Colonel Francis Charteris, who might aptly be termed (in Mr. Stead's phrase), the Minotaur of his day. It was he who renamed it after the home of his family in Nithsdale. As his exploits belong chiefly to London, we, fortunately, need not enlarge upon them here. The parricide already referred to was the murder of his father by Philip Standsfield. Sir James Standsfield had set up a cloth factory here, on the banks of the Tyne, and had done remarkably well. He had two sons, Philip and John. The eldest had been a scape-grace ever since that day when, as a student at St. Andrews, he had gone to a meeting-house and flung a loaf at the preacher. It took the astonished divine on the side of the head and aroused within him the spirit of prophecy. Addressing the crowded chapel at large (for the loaf had been thrown unseen from some dark corner), he saw in a vision the death of the culprit, at whose end there would be more present than were hearing him that day; " and the multitude then present," adds the chronicler, " was not small."

Philip had a short and ignominious military career on the Continent, and returned home to prey upon his father ; who, for sufficient reasons, disinherited him in favour of his younger brother. In the end, aided by some servants, he strangled the old man and threw the body in the river. For this he was‾ hanged at Edinburgh, and as the hanging was not effectual, the executioner had to finish by strangling him, in which public opinion of that time saw the neat handiwork of Providence.

XXXII

HERE begins Haddington, and here end good roads for the space of a mile ; and not until the burgh is left behind do they recommence. The traveller who might set out in quest of bad roads and vile paving would without difficulty discover the objects of his search at Haddington. He might conceivably find as bad elsewhere, but worse examples would be miraculous indeed. We have encountered many stretches of road, thus far, of a mediæval quality, but the long road to the North boasts, or blushes for, nothing nearly so craggy as are the cobble-stoned thoroughfares of this " royal burgh." The entrance to the town from the south resembles, in its picturesque squalor, that to one of the decayed towns of Brittany. Unswept, tatterdemalion as it is, it still remains a fitting subject for the artist's pencil, for here beside the narrow street stands the rugged mass of Bothwell Castle, patched and clouted from time to time, but happily as yet unrestored. Over the lintels of old houses adjoining, still remain the pious invocations and quaint devices originally sculptured there for the purpose of averting the baleful glance of the Evil Eye.

The initial letter in the name of Haddington is a superfluity and a misuse of the letter H, the name deriving from that of Ada, Countess of Northumberland and ancestress of Scottish monarchs ; foundress also of a nunnery here which has long gone the way of such mediæval things. The Tyne borders this town, and sometimes floods it, as may be readily seen by an inscription on the wall of a house in High Street, which tells how the water on October 4, 1775, suddenly rose eight feet and three quarters. A curious legend, too, still survives, recording a flood in 1358, when a mm of the pious Ada's old foundation, seizing a statue of the Virgin out of its niche, waded into the torrent and

BOTHWELL CASTLE.

threatened to throw it in unless the Blessed Mary instantly caused the waters to subside. That they immediately did so appears to have been taken as evidence of the effective moral suasion thus applied.

Haddington Abbey, the successor of earlier buildings, and now itself partly ruined, stands by the inconstant river, the nave, now the parish church, and the choir roofless, open to the sky. It is here within these grass-grown walls that " Jane Welsh Carlyle, spouse of Thomas Carlyle, Chelsea, London," lies, as the remorseful epitaph says, " suddenly snatched away from him, and the light of his life as if gone out." The spot where the Abbey stands, by the dishevelled and tumbledown quarter of Nungate, is the more abject now in that it

still possesses old mansions that tell of a more prosperous past.   Here, on the river-bank, neglected and
forlorn like everything around, is the fine old screen of
the Bowling Green, where no one has, for a century
past, played bowls, unless indeed the wraiths of bygone
Scottish notables haunt the spot o' nights and play
ghostly games, like the Kaatskill gnomes in *Rip Van
Winkle.*   It is from the other side of the river that the

HADDINGTON ABBEY, FROM NUNGATE.

Abbey is best seen, its roofless central tower, the
Lucernia Laudoniae, or " Lamp of Lothian," still
showing those triple lancets in every face which,
according to the legend, obtained for it that title.
To obtain this view, the Abbey bridge is crossed,
which even now vividly illustrates on its wall the ready
way the old burgh had with malefactors.   From it
projects a great hook, rusty for long want of usage,
from which were hanged the reivers, the horse-thieves,
and casual evildoers, with jurisdiction of the most
summary kind.   No Calcraft science with it either,
with neck broken in decent fashion, but just a hauling
up of the rope and a tying of it to some handy stanchion,
and the unhappy malefactor left to throttle by slow
degrees.   No other such picturesque hanging-place as

this, but what is scenery to a criminal about to be·
hanged like a tom-cat caught killing chickens.

The crest, arms, trade-mark or badge of Haddington
is a goat.   There is no doubt about that, for Billy
(or is it a Nanny ?) has his (or her) effigy on many
of the old buildings.   Only by comparison and by
slow degrees is it that the stranger arrives at the
conclusion that it is a goat, for the drawing of many
of these representations leaves much to be desired.
Some resemble an elephant, others a horse, others yet
what " the mind's eye, Horatio " might conceive a
Boojum to be like ; but in the open space where
High Street and Market Street join, the modern Market
Cross, surmounted by a more carefully executed
carving, determines the species.

This is the centre of the town and neater than its
entrance from the south.   The steepled classic building
close by is not a church but the Town House, masquerading in ecclesiastical disguise, very much as
Berwick's Town Hall does.   From this point it is only
seventeen miles into Edinburgh ; but in 1750 and for
long after the coach journey employed the best efforts
of the local stage during the whole day.   Musselburgh,
little more than eleven miles away, was reached in time
for dinner, and only when evening was come did the
lumbering vehicle lurch into its destination in Auld
Reekie, when every one went to bed, bruised and weary
with the toils of the expedition.   The road at that time
must have resembled the specimen of roadway still
adorning the south entrance to Haddington.

To-day, happily, it is in good condition as far as
Levenhall, seven miles short of our journey's end,
whence it is bad beyond the credibility of those who
have not seen it.   Gladsmuir, Macmerry, and Tranent
are interposed between ; places that sink their memories
of the battle of Prestonpans in ironfounding and coal-
digging and suchlike, disregarding the futilities of the
Stuarts.   As for Macmerry, whose name prefigures
orgies at the most of it, or sober revelry at the very
least, it is odds against your finding as depressing a place

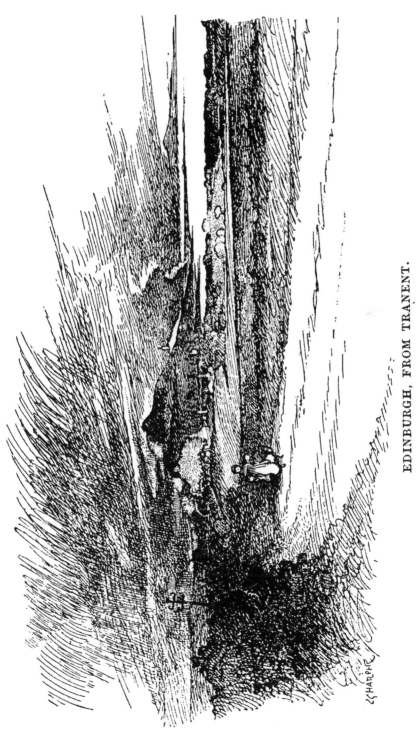

EDINBURGH, FROM TRANENT.

within a hundred miles. If place-names were made to fit, why, then, Macdolour might suit it to a marvel. Why ? Just because it stands at the crest of a barren knowe ; an ugly row of cottages on either side, with cinders and dust, clinkers and mud in front of them, and some gaunt works within eyeshot. God knows who christened the place, or if the name signified merriment, but, if it did, either the scene has changed wholly since then, or else he was a humorist of the sardonic sort who so dubbed it. Tranent, too, a townlet subsisting upon collieries : how grimly commonplace ! But it at least has this advantage, that from its elevated foothold it looks down upon the Firth of Forth, that noble frith which Victor Hugo blundered over so whimsically in rendering it as " *la Première de la Quatrième.*" Seen under the summer sun, how glorious that seaward view, with the villages of Preston and Cockenzie, half hidden by their woodlands, by the level shores. Half-way down from Tranent's hillside you see a fine panorama : Arthur's Seat in front, Calton Hill and its Nelson's column, peering from behind, and the distant shores of Fife, with blowing smoke-clouds, many miles away. Between Arthur's Seat and the Calton, Edinburgh is hid, nine miles from this point. Down in the levels in the mid-distance there are hints of Musselburgh in smoke-wreaths and peeping towers ; and mayhap, while you gaze, the southward-bound train, with its white puff of steam, is seen setting forth on its long journey. Londonwards. In these levels was fought the battle of Prestonpans, Sunday, September 21, 1745, around that village of Preston and those briny meads where the salt-pans used to be and are no longer.

Preston—formerly Priest's Town—got its name at the time when it was part of the celebrated Abbey of Newbattle. The monks of that religious house were the first discoverers of coal in Scotland, and also, in the twelfth century, made this district the seat of a manufacture of salt. Prestonpans, indeed, at one time supplied the whole of the East Coast with salt, and it was only on the repeal of the Salt Duty that this old town fell into decay. Women, known as salt-wives, a class almost as picturesque as the _ fish-wives of Newhaven, used to carry the salt in creels on their backs, to sell in Edinburgh and other towns.

In an orchard stands what was once the ancient village cross, erected in 1617, in place of an earlier. Well-known as the " Chapmen's Cross," it was the meeting-place of the chapmen, packmen, or pedlars of the Lothians. They gathered early in July, transacted the business of their guild and elected their " King " and his " Lord Deputy " for the ensuing year. The " ink-bottle," cut in stone, into which they dipped their pens, is still visible on the base of the cross. The Bannatyne Club saved it from utter destruction, and instituted a convivial guild, the " Society of Chapmen of the Lothians," visiting the cross every year, with Sir Walter Scott as one of their members.

The world has vastly changed since " the Forty-five." It has, as a small detail, ceased to produce its salt by evaporation of sea water ; and, a larger and more significant matter, no longer wages war for sake of dynasties. The Highlanders who fought and gained this fleeting victory for Prince Charlie were the last who drew the sword for Romance and Right Divine. Prince Charlie had moved out of his loyal Edinburgh at the approach of the English under Sir John Cope, who, of course, in that fine foolish manner of British officers, which will survive as long as the officers themselves, wholly underrated his enemy. He was defeated easily, with every circumstance of indignity, his soldiers fleeing in abject terror before the impetuous charge of the ferocious hairy-legged Highlanders, emerging, figures of grotesque horror, out of the mists slowly dispersing off the swampy fields in the laggard September sunrise.

The English numbered 2100 against the 1400 under Prince Charlie ; but only four minutes passed between the attack and the flight. In that short space of time

Q

the field was deserted and the clansmen, pursuing the terror-stricken rabble which just before had been a disciplined force, slew nearly four hundred of them. The total loss of the Highlanders in slain was thirty, nearly the whole of them falling in the first discharge of musketry. Almost incredible, but well-authenticated, stories are told of the cowardice of Cope's regiments. Cope himself was swept away in the wild rush, vainly endeavouring to stem it, and it was not until they were two miles from the field, at St. Clement's Wells, that he could bring them to a halt. Even then, the accidental discharge of a pistol scared them off again, and although no one pursued, they rode off with redoubled energy. This precipitate retreat of mounted troops over miles of country, from an unmounted enemy who were not pursuing them, is perhaps the most disgraceful incident in the military history of the country. .

The flying infantry were in far worse case. In endeavouring to escape by climbing the park walls of Preston, they were cut down in great numbers by the terrible broadswords of the Highlanders. Colonel Gardiner and a brave few were cut down defending themselves on the field of battle. One story, of a piece with many others, relates how a Highlander, pursuing alone a party of ten soldiers, struck down the hinder-most with his sword, and shouting, " Down with your arms ! " called upon the others to surrender. They threw their weapons away without looking behind them, and the Highlander, his sword in one hand and a pistol in the other, drove them—nine of them !— prisoners into camp. Everywhere Cope, so helter-skelter was his flight, himself brought the first news of his defeat. He reached Coldstream that night, and did not rest until the next day he was within the sheltering fortifications of Berwick.

We will not further pursue the fortunes of the Young Pretender, but hurry on into Levenhall.

Where that battle was fought, there is to-day the most extensive cabbage-plant cultivation in Scotland. It is a usual thing in the early part of the year for almost daily special cabbage trains to be despatched to all parts of Britain.

And so downhill, and then over the awful cobbles into the accursed town of Musselburgh. "Accursed," not by reason of those self-same cobbles, but for the sacrilegious doings of its magistrates who rebuilt their Tolbooth, burnt after the battle of Pinkie, with stones from the Chapel of Loretto. Now that chapel, which stood at the entrance to the town, was the place of business of one of those roadside hermits of whom we have in these pages heard so much (would that he had a successor in these times, for then the road would perhaps be in better condition), and the Pope, indignant at the injury done to the wayside shrine, solemnly anathematised town and inhabitants in sleeping or waking, eating and drinking, at every conceivable time and every imaginable function. No Pope since that period seems to have removed the curse, and no one is particularly anxious that it should be removed, Musselburgh being rather proud of it than otherwise. When it begins to take effect will be quite time enough. There were those who at the close of the coaching days perceived the beginning of it, although then three hundred years overdue, but as the town has rather increased in prosperity since that period, the time evidently is not yet. Nor do the burghers anticipate it, for they still repeat the brave old rhyme :—

> Musselburgh was a burgh
> When Edinburgh was nane ;
> And Musselburgh shall be a burgh
> When Edinburgh is gane.

This, however, is a quibble, for Musselburgh derived its name from the "broch," or bed, of mussels at the mouth of the river Esk. Looked at in this light, the statement is true enough and the prophecy a not particularly rash one. The sponsorial shell-fish have an honoured place in the town arms, in which three mussels are seen in company with three anchors : the motto "Honesty" writ large below. This was probably adopted at some period later than the purloining of the stones of the Loretto Chapel.

The Town Hall, with that tower whose building brought about the curse, forms the centre of Mussel-burgh, a fishy, stony, picturesque place with four bridges over the Esk, leading to the western bank,

MUSSELBURGH.

where the fisher quarter of Fisherrow straggles towards Joppa, two miles distant. Joppa Pans are gone now, just as those other pans at Preston, but factories of sorts, with clustered chimney-stacks, are still grouped about the melancholy sea-shore, where gales set the very high-road awash on occasion. Not vulgar, modern factories, but of a certain age ; old enough and grim enough to look like the scene of some thrilling story that yet awaits the telling. Somewhat thrilling is the report as to the condition of the road here in 1680, a complaint laid before the Privy Council stating that, four miles on the London side of Edinburgh, travelling was dangerous, and travellers to be pitied, " either by their coaches overturning, their horses falling, their carts breaking, their loads casting, or horses stumbling, and the poor people with burdens on their backs sorely discouraged ; moreover, strangers do often exclaim thereat." All this reads with a very modern touch to those who know the road to-day, for it is as bad now as it could have been then, and so continues, in different kinds of badness, through adjoining Portobello into Edinburgh itself. Here seas of slimy mud, there precipitous setts, here again profound holes in the macadam, or tramway rails projecting above the road level, make these last miles wretched. Portobello, that suburban seaside resort of Edinburgh, fares in this respect no better than the rest of the way, and the original road across Figgate Whins, the lonely moor that was here before the first house of Portobello was built, could have been no worse. That house was the creation of a retired sailor who had been at the capture of Portobello in Central America by Admiral Vernon in 1739. He named it after that town, and when the present seaside resort began to spring up, it took the title. Now it has a promenade, a pier, hotels, and crowds of visitors in summer upon the sands, and calls itself " the Brighton of Scotland." Observe that Brighton does not return the compliment, and has not yet begun to style itself " the Portobello of England."

XXXIII

LEAVING the " Brighton of Scotland " behind, we come to the flat lands of Craigentinny, stretching away from the now suburban highway down to the wind-swept and desolate seashore, where the whaups and the sandpipers make mournful concerts in a minor key, to the accompaniment of the noise of the sullen breakers and the soughing of the wind amid the rustling bents. Overlooking the road, within sight and sound of the tinkling tramcars passing between Joppa, Portobello, and Edinburgh, is that singular monument, " Miller's Tomb."

William Henry Miller, whose remains lie beneath this pile of classic architecture, was an antiquary and bibliophile, and obtained his nickname of " Measure

Miller " from his habit of measuring the margins of the " tall copies " of the scarce books he bought. His beardless face and shrill voice led to the lifelong belief the he was really a woman. The tomb is elaborately decorated with a carved marble frieze representing the Song of Miriam and the destruction of the Egyptians in the Red Sea. Miller and his father were both Quakers, and the wealth of which they were possessed derived from a prosperous seedsman's business in Canongate, Edinburgh. To the father came an adventure which does not fall to many men. He was married in 1789 for the third time, when nearly seventy years of age, to an Englishwoman, who conveyed him against his will in a post-chaise from Edinburgh to London.

Passing Craigentinny and Jock's Lodge we are, in the words of the old song, " Within a mile of Edinburgh town." The more modern and acceptable name of Jock's Lodge is Piershill, but it has been known by the other for over two hundred and seventy years. Who the original Jock was seems open to doubt, but he is supposed to have been a beggar who built himself a hut on this then lonely road leading to Figgate Whins. Even in 1650, when Cromwell besieged Edinburgh, the spot had obtained its name, and is referred to as " that place called Jockis Lodge." Towards the close of the eighteenth century a Colonel Piers had a villa here, pulled down in 1793, when barracks—known as Piershill Barracks—were built on the site. It is a district slowly emerging from the reproach of a disreputable past, when footpads and murderers haunted the muddy roads, or took refuge amid the towering rocks of Arthur's Seat, Crow Hill, or Salisbury Craigs, or hid in the congenial sloughs of the Hunter's Bog. Close by the road, at the entrance to the Queen's Park of Holyrood, is Muschat's Cairn, the place where Scott makes Jeanie Deans meet the outlaw Robertson. This heap of stones marks the spot where Nicol Muschat of Boghall, a surgeon, a man of infamous character, murdered his wife by cutting her throat in 1720, a crime which, with Scottish old-time mysticism, he said was committed by direct personal instigation of the devil. All the same, they hanged him for it in the Grassmarket, where martyrs " testified " of old and the criminals of " Auld Reekie " expiated their crimes.

Of course the approach to Edinburgh has, from the picturesque standpoint, been spoiled. Ranges of grim stone houses and sprawling suburbs now hem in the road and hide the view of Arthur's Seat and its neighbouring eminences ; but a few steps to the left serve to disclose them, the little loch of St. Margaret, and the ruined walls of St. Anthony's Chapel on the hillside, once guarding the holy well. St. Anthony's Chapel, within the rule of the Abbey of Holyrood, served another turn, for from its tower glimmered a beacon which in the old days guided mariners safely up the Forth, a service paid for out of the harbour dues.

The so-called " London " and " Regent " Roads that now lead directly into the New Town of Edinburgh are modern improvements upon the old approach through Canongate into the Old Town. If steep, rugged, and winding, the old way was at least more impressive, for it lay within sight of Holyrood Palace and brought the wayfarer into the very heart of Scott's " own romantic town," to where the smells and the dirt, the crazy tenement-houses and the ragged clouts hanging from dizzy tiers of windows, showed " Scotia's darling seat " in its most characteristic aspects.

As Alexander Smith puts it, Scott discovered the city was beautiful, sang its praises to the world, " and he has put more coin into the pockets of its inhabitants than if he had established a branch of manufacture of which they had the monopoly."

The distant view of Edinburgh is magnificent. The peaked and jagged masses of Arthur's Seat and Salisbury Craigs, the monument-cumbered Calton Hill, the Castle Rock—all these combine to make the traveller eager to reach so picturesque a spot. Approaching it and seeing the smoke-cloud drifting with the breeze away from the hollow from which Edinburgh's million chimneys are seen peering, one instantly notes the peculiar appropriateness of the Scots endearing epithet, " Auld Reekie." But it was not only—if indeed at all—an admiration of the picturesque that made the sight of Edinburgh so welcome to old-time travellers. It was rather the prospect of coming to the end of their journey, and almost in sight of a comfortable hotel, that rendered

CALTON HILL.

the view so welcome to those who in the last thirty years or so of the coaching era made this trip of almost four hundred miles ; but those who had come this way at an earlier period had no such comfortable prospect before them. Instead of putting up at some fine hospitable inn, such as they were used to even in the smaller English towns, they were set down at a " stabler's," the premises of one whose first business was to horse the coaches and to let saddle-horses, and who, as in some sort of an after-thought, lodged those who were obliged to journey about the country.

A traveller arriving at Edinburgh in 1774, for
instance, had indeed little comfort awaiting him.
" One can scarcely form in imagination the distress
of a miserable stranger on his first entrance into this
city," says one writing at this period.   No inn better
than an alehouse, no decent or cleanly accommodation,
nor in fact anything fit for a gentleman.   " On my
first arrival," says this traveller, " my companion
and self, after the fatigue of a long day's journey, were
landed at one of these stable-keepers' (for they have
modesty to give themselves no higher denomination) in
a part of the town which is called the Pleasance ; and
on entering the house we were conducted by a poor girl
without shoes or stockings, and with only a single
linsey-woolsey petticoat which just reached half-way to
her ankles, into a room where about twenty Scotch
drovers had been regaling themselves with whisky and
potatoes.   You may guess our amazement when we
were informed that this was the best inn in the metro-
polis, and that we could have no beds unless we had an
inclination to sleep together, and in the same room with
the company which a stage-coach had that moment
discharged.   ' Well,' said I to my friend, ' there is
nothing like seeing men and manners ; perhaps we
may be able to repose ourselves at some coffee-house.'
Accordingly, on inquiry, we discovered that there was
a good dame by the Cross who acted in the double
capacity of pouring out coffee and letting lodgings to
strangers, as we were.   She was easily to be found out,
and, with all the conciliating complaisance of a
Maîtresse d'Hôtel, conducted us to our destined apartments, which were indeed six stories high, but so
infernal in appearance that you would have thought
youserlf in the regions of Erebus.   The truth is, I will
venture to say, you will make no scruple to believe
when I tell you that in the whole we had only two
windows, which looked into an alley five feet wide,
where the houses were at least ten stories high and the
alley itself was so sombre in the brightest sunshine that
it was impossible to see any object distinctly."

Private lodgings, just as those described above, were the resort of those who had neither friends nor acquaintance in Edinburgh at that time ; but travellers in Scotland were nearly always exercising their ingenuity to come, at the end of their day's journey, to the house of some friend or some friend's friend, to whom before starting they had been careful to obtain letters of introduction. So old and so widespread a custom was this that, so far back as 1425, we find an Act of James the First of Scotland actually forbidding all travellers resorting to burgh towns to lodge with friends or acquaintances, or in any place but the " hostillaries," unless indeed he was a personage of consequence, with a great retinue, in which case he might accept a friend's hospitality, provided that his " horse and meinze " were sent to the inns.

Of course such an Act was doomed to fall into neglect, but the innkeepers, equally of course during a long series of years, almost ceased to exist. A few " stablers' " establishments became known as " inns " at about the period of Doctor Johnson's visit to Edinburgh. They were chiefly situated in the Pleasance, or in that continuation of it, St. Mary's Wynd (now St. Mary Street). These inns, such as they were, burst upon the by no means delighted gaze of the wayfarer from England as he entered the historic town of Edinburgh, and when he saw them he generally lifted up his voice and cursed the fate that had sent him so far from home and into so barbarous a country.

The Pleasance was largely in receipt of the traffic to and from the south until the construction of the North and South Bridges, opened in 1769 and 1788, diverted it to a higher level. We may look in vain nowadays in the Pleasance for the inns of that day. They are demolished and altered so greatly as to be unrecognisable ; but the " White Horse," which stands in a court away down Canongate, will give us an idea of the kind of place. Situated in " White Horse," or Davison's Close in Canongate, and reached from that street by a low-browed archway, it remains a

perfect example of the Edinburgh inn of nearly three
hundred years ago.   An inn no longer, but occupied
in tenements, the internal arrangements are somewhat
altered, but the time when the house extended a

THE " WHITE HORSE " INN.

primitive hospitality to travellers is not difficult to
reconstruct in the imagination.   To it, at the end
of their journeys, came those wearied ones, to find
accommodation of the most intimate and domestic
kind.   Kitchen and dining-room were one, and it
was scarce possible for a guest to obtain a bedroom
to himself.   Dirt was accepted as inevitable.   In
fact, the modern " dosser " is better and more decently
housed.   To the " White Horse " came others—those
about to set out upon their travels.   Booted and
spurred, wills made and saddle-bags packed, they
resorted hither to hire horses for their journeys, and
it is not unlikely that the old house saw in early
times many a quaking laird, badly wanted by the

Government, slinking through the archway from the Canongate, to secure trusty mounts for instant flight. Scott, indeed, has made it the scene of strange doings in his *Waverley.*

This is the oldest house in Edinburgh ever used as an inn, but must not be confused with that other " White Horse," long since demolished, made famous by Doctor Johnson.

It was in 1773 that Johnson reached Edinburgh. He put up at the " White Horse " in Boyd's Close, called, even in those uncleanly times, " that dirty and dismal " inn, kept by James Boyd. The great man immediately notified his arrival to Boswell in this short note :—

" *Saturday night.*—Mr. Johnson sends his compliments to Mr. Boswell, being just arrived at Boyd's."

When Boswell arrived, falling over himself in his eagerness, he found the Doctor furiously angry. Doubtless he had been conducted to his room, as was not unusually the case, by some dirty sunburnt wench, without shoes or stockings, a fit object for dislike ; but the chief cause of his anger was the waiter, who had sweetened his lemonade without the ceremony of using the sugar-tongs. He threw the lemonade out of window, and seemed inclined to throw the waiter after it.

" Peter Ramsay's " was a famous inn, situated at the foot of St. Mary's Wynd, next the Cowgate Port. To it came travellers along both the east and the south roads. Ramsay advertised it in 1776 as being " a good house for entertainment, good stables for above one hundred horses, and sheds for about twenty carriages." In 1790, he retired with a fortune of £10,000. But in the best of these old Edinburgh inns the beds well merited a description given of them as " dish-clouts stretched on grid-irons."

First among the innkeepers of this unsanctified quarter to remove from it into the New Town was James Dun. He was a man notable among his kind, having not only been the first to call himself an

" innkeeper " instead of a " stabler," but the greatly daring person who first used the outlandish word " Hotel " in Edinburgh. He began " hotel "-keeping in the flats above the haberdashery shop of John Neale, who, two years before, in 1774, had built the first house in the New Town. Neale himself was a pioneer of considerable nerve, for although the New Town had been projected and building-sites laid out on what is now the chief ornament of it, Princes Street, prospective tenants were shy of so bleak and exposed a situation as this then was. They preferred to live in the dirty cosiness of the old wynds and closes, and so the New Town seemed likely to be a paper project for years to come. At this juncture the Town Council made a sporting offer of exemption from all local taxes for the first who would build a house there. Neale was this pioneer, and he built the house that still stands next the Register House, the most easterly house in Princes Street.

Dun, to whom he had let the upper part, immediately displayed a great gilded sign, " Dun's Hotel," whereupon the Lord Provost, representing public feeling, wrote objecting to the foreign word " Hotel," saying that, whatever might be the *real* character of his establishment, he might at least avoid the scandalous indecency of publicly proclaiming it !

XXXIV

THESE concluding pages of a book on the road to Edinburgh form no fitting place to attempt the description or history of so ancient and historic a town. Our business is to reach the northern capital, leaving the story of Edwin's Burgh to be told by others. Yet we cannot leave it thus without some brief survey.

The modern traveller by road, coming in by the London Road, Greenside, Leith Street, and Princes Street, comes in by the New Town, and sees on his

"SQUALOR AND PICTURESQUENESS."

left, across a deep ravine, partly occupied by a huge railway station and partly by beautiful public gardens, the dark mass of the Castle and the Old Town crowning the opposite heights, grey and stern, in effective contrast with the gay flower-beds down below, the old houses huddling together on the scanty foothold of the ridge and rising to sheer heights. *That* is the original historic town : *this*, to which the modern traveller comes by road, the new. Little more than a hundred years ago this New Town was not thought of : its site the meadows and wastes that sloped down to the Firth of Forth and the sea, and the site of the railway station and the Princes Street Gardens covered with the dark waters of the Nor' Loch.

Old-time arrivals in Edinburgh, coming in by Canongate, found themselves in midst of squalor and pictur-esqueness ;   and

although much of the picturesque is gone, it is still
a quaint street and the squalor survives. The
poor who live here " hang forth their banners from
the outward walls," in the shape of their domestic

CANONGATE.

washing, fluttering in the breeze from every window,
at the end of long poles, and how poor they are
may be judged from the condition of the clothes
they consider worth keeping. That sometime prison,
the Canongate Tolbooth, facing the long street, remains
one of the most curious relics of Edinburgh's past.

Not a very ancient past, for it was only " biggit " in 1591, but old enough to be regarded with reverence, and quaint to admiration, with its spired tower and tourelles, so eminently Scotch of that period when the French influence in architecture was yet strong. You can match those curious spires time and time again among the old châteaux of the Loire, and in Brittany ; just as in the old Norman town of Coutances one can find the counterpart of the old theatre in Playhouse Close, near by.

From here, those travellers saw the Old Town ahead and, progressing up High Street, came successively to the Tron Church, the Market Cross, St. Giles's Cathedral, and, before 1817—when it was pulled down—to the Old Tolbooth. Beyond this, the Lawnmarket conducted to the Castle, which then marked the end of the town. In this progress the tall and crowded houses and darkening wynds and closes stood to right and left. Later years have seen the disappearance of many of these places, where in old times the ferocious Scots nobles lived, poor and proud, bloodthirsty and superstitious, but those that are left are very grim, dark, and dirty, and the ten- and eleven-storied houses of such a height that only by great exertions is it possible to crane the neck and lift the eyes to the skyline, against which the belching chimneys of the piled-up " lands " are projecting the smoke of domestic hearths and eternally justifying the old Scots term of endearment for Edinburgh. The nobles are gone, lang syne, their old dens occupied now by the very poorest of Edinburgh's poor ; but sanitary conditions, even with the present occupants, are not so degraded as they were when the flower of Scotland's nobility dwelt here ; when pigs and fowls were herded in the basements, or ran unheeded in the alleys, and wayfarers skulked under the walls at the sound of voices above, calling " gardy-loo "—a call which accompanied a discharge of overflowing house-hold utensils from inconceivable heights into the gutters below. " Gardy-loo " was a term which, with this dreadfully unclean custom, derived from France, having been originally *gardez-l'eau ;* just as the cakes sold at Craigmillar, called "petticoat tails" were originally *petits gateaux.*

Still, the Old Town is sufficiently grimy and huddled yet to fitly illustrate the Scottish saying "The clartier (i.e. the dirtier) the cosier."

Nothing is more characteristic of the Old Town than the religious texts carved upon the stone door lintels of these ancient houses. Few are without them. To a stranger they would seem to tell of a fervent piety, but they meant more than that. They were always

OLD INSCRIPTION, LADY STAIR'S HOUSE.

accompanied with a date and with the initials—sometimes also the arms—of their owners; as in the beautiful example still remaining in Lady Stair's Close, and represented both pride and a fearful superstition. Superstition, because the improving texts and pious ejaculations meant little beyond talismanic protection against "Auld Hornie," wizards, and warlocks, wehrwolves, and all those frightful inhabitants of Satan's invisible world in which the Scotch most fervently believed, from king to peasant. Thus when we read over one of these old doorways the queerly spelled

Blissit be God in all His giftis,

we know that this was little less than an incantation, and marked a lively sense of favours to come; and when our eye lights upon the inscription next door,

|Pax intrantibus : Salus exevntibvs,

R

we know that the good feeling thus prominently displayed would by no means have prevented the fierce lord of the house from stabbing his guest in a dark corner, if he had a mind to it.

A highly interesting book might be written on these old sculptured stones alone. Nor are they in every instance old. Some modern ones exist, and the entirely laudable passion for commemoration has caused interesting tablets to be set up, marking many of Edinburgh's famous spots. A curious modern piece of sculpture decorates more or less artistically the archway leading from the High Street into Paisley Close, supporting a tall building erected in 1862. It represents the bust of a boy, and includes an inscribed label. It seems that the old building standing on this site suddenly collapsed on a Sunday morning in 1861, and buried a number of

THE "HEAVE AWA" SIGN.

people in the ruins, thirty-five actually dying from their injuries. Some were fortunate enough to be screened from the heavy masses of stone and brick by timbers which in falling had imprisoned them. Among these was the lad whose face is represented in the carving. The rescuers who came with pick and shovel to dig out the survivors had succoured many, and were turning back when they heard the muffled cry, " Heave awa, lads, I'm no' deid yet," and redoubling their efforts, extricated the author of it.

No relic now remains upon the door-posts of these old houses of the curious contrivance which preceded the door-knocker, and for the sight of a "tirle-pin" the stranger must needs go to the museum of the Royal Scottish Society of Antiquaries, to which the last example was long since removed, from an old house in the Canongate.

The tirle-pin had a variety of names. Sometimes it would be called a " risp " or a " ringle," and there were those who knew it as a " craw " ; that is to say, a crow, from the harsh crow-like sound produced by its use. A tirle-pin was just a rasping contrivance made of a twisted bar of iron fixed against the door post with an iron ring hanging loosely from it, as in the accompanying sketch. Instead of knocking, one who desired admittance would seize the ring and rasp it up and down the twisted iron, producing a noise which could be distinctly heard within.

The origin of the tirle-pin, like that of many another Scottish custom, was French. It originated in France in the times of the Valois, in days when it was not etiquette to knock at the doors of royal personages. In face of this, courtiers were reduced to scratching with the finger-nails—a disagreeable sensation when practised upon wood, as any one who tries it may readily discover for himself. Perhaps from this cause, or because the scratching was not loud enough (or, perhaps, even because the polish began to disappear from the royal portals) this mechanical scratcher was invented. The fashion spread from France to Scotland in times when the two countries were linked in close ties of friendship. From the palace it spread down to the mansions of the nobles and the houses of the merchants, finally coming into general use. It was never acclimatised in England, although another kind of scratching was, if we may believe the satirists, who say that James the First and his Scottish followers imported the itch.

A TIRLE-PIN.

However, the **tirle-pin** is obsolete, but it did not disappear without leaving a trace of its existence in old Scots ballads ; as, for instance, that of *Sweet William's Ghaist* :—

> There cam a ghaist to Margaret's door,
>   Wi' mony a grievous groan :
> And aye he tirled upon the pinne,
>   But answer made she nane.
>
> Is that my father Philip ?
>   Or is't my brother John,
> Or is't my true love Willie
>   To Scotland now come hame ?

XXXV

A GRIM old town, Edinburgh, dominated by the ancient castle from its rock, bodeful with the story of a thousand years. Newer new towns have sprung up around it to south and west, and hem the old fortress in with a bordure of unhistoric suburbs, so that from the topmost battlements you see how small the original Edinburgh is, compared with its surroundings. Places of pilgrimage are not lacking in the old streets. There are John Knox's house, one of the queerest, three-storied, and gabled, the very ideal of rugged strength ; and the Parliament Square, once St. Giles's churchyard, where " I K 1572," on a stone in the pavement, marks the site of Knox's grave. Passers-by walk over it, curiously fulfilling Johnson's aspiration, made years before the churchyard was destroyed, by which he hoped that the dour Presbyterian was buried on a highway. While we are on the subject of tombs, let us mention that other place of pilgrimage, Greyfriars churchyard, that grisly place where Robert Louis Stevenson was accustomed in his youth to make assignations with parlour-maids. Few places so grim as a Scottish burial-ground, and Greyfriars is of these the grimmest. Dishevelled backs of houses look down upon the mouldering tombs, and kitchens and living-rooms open into the houses of the dead. Rusty iron railings, bolts and bars, guard the blackened and broken mausoleums and give the pilgrim the weird idea that the living have taken extraordinary precautions to imprison those who are never likely to break

GREYFRIARS.

out. The only living things here are the foul grass that grows within the sepulchral enclosures, and the demon cats of an heraldic slimness that haunt the churchyard in incredible numbers, and stealing victuals from the neighbouring houses, gnaw them within the tombs. Many martyrs for religion have their resting-place here, together with those who martyr̂d them. Persecutors and persecuted alike rest here now.

Sympathies will ever be divided between the Covenanters and their oppressors. As you read how they upheld their faith and signed their names to the Covenant in this gruesome yard of Greyfriars, so ominously on that flat tombstone which even now remains, you are fired with an enthusiasm for those rejecters of a liturgy alien from their convictions, and can curse " Claverse " with the best of those who do not forget the heavy ways of " bonnie Dundee " with them. But the Covenanters were as intolerant with those when they came to rule. The men of both sides were men of blood. The strain of intolerance remains, and the tomb of that other persecutor of the Covenan-ters, Sir George Mackenzie, has always been, and still is, with the people " bloody Mackenzie's."

Old Edinburgh life centred at the Market Cross, happily restored in 1885 by Mr. Gladstone. The Cross has had a troubled history. Reconstructed from a much older one in 1617, it remained here until 1756, when the " improving " fanatics of that time swept the historic structure away, without a thought of the associations belonging to it. They were associations of every kind. Kings had been proclaimed at it by heralds. with fanfare of trumpet ; patriots and traitors with equal contumely had been done to death beside it ; and the continual round of punishments which gave the common hangman a busy time were inflicted here. In fact, were a rogue to be pilloried or a king's birthday to be kept with becoming ceremony, the Cross was the place. Let us see what those punishments were like, from one example illustrative of the general run of them. Here is what they did in 1655 to " Mr. Patrik Maxwell, ane arrant decevar." They brought him here " quhair a pillorie wes erectit, gairdit and convoyed with a company of sodgeris; and their, eftir ane full houris standing on that pillorie, with his heid and handis lyand out and hoilis cuttit out for that end, his rycht lug was cuttit af; and thaireftir careyit over to the town of St. Johnnestoun, qubair ane uther pillorie wes erectit, on the quhilk the uther left lug wes cuttit af him. The caus heirof wes this; that he haid gevin out fals calumneis and leyis aganes Collonell Daniell, governour of Peirth. Bot the treuth is, he was ane notorious decevar and ane intelligencer, sumtyme for the Englesches, uther tymes for the Scottis, and decevand both of thame: besyde mony prankis quhilk wer tedious to writt." Quite so; but if all de-ceivers had their ears cut off, how few would retain them! A ferocious folk, those old Scots, and petty

THE WOODEN HORSE.

delinquents supped sorrow at their hands with a big spoon. Sorry the lot of scandal-mongers and the like, seated on a wooden horse with hands and legs tied, and permission freely accorded to all for the throwing of missiles. Ferocity, however, should go hand in hand with courage—a quality apparently not possessed by the citizens of Edinburgh when Prince Charlie and his Highlanders came, in 1745. Incredulous of the wild clansmen ever daring to attack the town, they laughed at the very idea; but when they heard of his small force having eluded the force of Johnny Cope, sent to intercept them, and advancing in earnest, things took a very different colour. Those who were loyal to the House of Hanover were quaking in their shoes, and the Jacobites rejoicing. The city armed, even to the clergymen, who, on the Sunday before the surrender, preached in the churches with swords and daggers buckled on under their gowns.   Bands of volunteers were raised, and on the report that the Pretender was near, were marched outside the walls to dispute his entry, despite their murmurs that they had volunteered to defend the city from the inside, and were not prepared to go out to be cut to pieces with the invaders' claymores.   Captain ex-Provost Drummond marched with his company down the West Bow towards the West Port.   Looking round when he had reached it, he to his astonishment found himself alone.   The volunteers had vanished down the back lanes or closes ! But the dragoons were as bad.   Coming near the enemy at Corstorphine, two miles out, they bolted without firing a shot, and so back into Edinburgh and through it and out at the other end.   It was the ferocious appearance of the Highlanders that caused this terror.   They were comparatively few ; ill-armed, ragged, and ill-fed.   But their strange dress, their wild looks, shaggy locks, and generally outlandish appearance, frightened the good Lowlanders, who knew almost as little of these Gaelic tribes as Londoners themselves.   The old-time warfare of the Japanese and the Chinese, with their hideous masks ; the dismal tom-toming of the African savage ; the war-paint of the Red Indian, are justified of their existence, for the strange and hideous in warfare is very effective in striking a paralysing terror into an enemy.   Accordingly, the tartans, the naked legs and arms, and the uncombed locks of the lairds' uncivilised levies captured Edinburgh for Prince Charlie, who, a few days later, September 17, caused his father, the Old Pretender, to be proclaimed king, by the title of James the Third, at the Cross.

With the suppression of " the Forty-five," the stirring warlike story of Edinburgh came to an end ; but not until 1807, when the Edinburgh police came into existence, was the semi-military Town Guard, raised in 1682, abolished.   The Town Guard and the towns-

STATELY PRINCES STREET.

people were always at odds, and hated one another cordially. Recruited from the army, and armed with the formidable weapons called " Jeddart axes," it was

THE LAST OF THE
TOWN GUARD.

originally a fine body, designed rather to keep the town in order than to protect it, and its members never lost sight of that fact. In its last years, however, the Town Guard declined in importance and in numbers, and, coming to be regarded as a refuge for old pensioners who could scarcely manage to crawl about, became an object of derision. *Then* the sins of their forerunners were visited upon the heads of those unhappy old men, and it became a common sight to see them baited by mischievous small boys. The last of the Town Guard tottered about Parliament Square in his queer uniform and three-cornered hat, hardly able to shoulder his axe, and regarded by the inhabitants as one of their most genuine antiquities, until he too followed his comrades to the tomb.

XXXVI

ONE must needs admire Edinburgh. You may have seen the noblest cities of the world; have stood upon the Acropolis at Athens, on the Heights of Abraham at Quebec; have viewed Rome and her seven hills, or Constantinople from the Goldern Horn; but Edinburgh still retains her pride of place, even in the eyes of the much travelled. You need not be Scottish to feel the charm of her, and can readily understand why she means so much to the Scot; but your gorge rises at the immemorial dirt of the Old Town, simultaneously

EDINBURGH, NEW TOWN, 1847 FROM MONS MEG BATTERY. *By David Roberts, R.A.*

with your admiration of its wondrous picturesqueness, and stately Princes Street seems to you a revelation of magnificence even while the bulk of the New Town appears grey, formal, and forbidding. The great gulf fixed between Old Town and New, that ravine in which the railway burrows, and on whose banks the Princes Street Gardens run, renders that thoroughfare, with its one side of grass and trees and the other of fine shops and towering houses, reminiscent to the Londoner of Piccadilly. But Piccadilly has not a towering Castle on one side of it, nor a Calton Hill at the end ; nor, on the other hand, does Piccadilly know such easterly blasts as those that sweep down the long length of Princes Street and freeze the very marrow of the Southerner.

" The same isothermal line," wrote Robert Chambers, " passes through Edinburgh and London." " Still," James Payn used to say, " I never knew of a four-wheeled cab being blown over by an east wind in London, as has just happened in Edinburgh," and R.L.S. tells us frankly that his native city has " the vilest climate under heaven."

Princes Street is perhaps even more like the Brighton Front in its well-dressed crowds and fine shops. With the sea in place of the Gardens and the Castle, the resemblance would be singularly close.

As for Calton Hill, that neo-classic eminence, gives form and substance to Edinburgh's claim to be the " Modern Athens." Learning had not been unknown in the Old Town, where Hume and Boswell wrote ; but, given air and elbow-room, it expanded vastly when the New Town was planned, and with the dawn of the nineteenth century, literature flourished exceedingly. This seems to have inspired the idea of emulating the capital of Greece, to the eye as well as to the mind. Accordingly a copy of the Parthenon was begun on the crest of Calton Hill, as a monument to the Scots soldiers who fell in the campaigns against Napoleon. It cost a huge sum and has never been completed, and so it has familiarly been called

" Scotland's Folly " and " Scotland's Shame " ; but doubtless looks a great deal more impressive in its unfinished state, in the semblance of a ruin, than it would were it ever finished. A variety of other freak buildings keep it company : the Nelson Monument, memorials to Burns, to Dugald Stewart, and to Professor Playfair, together with what the many " guides," who by some phenomenal instinct scent the stranger from afar, call an " obsairvatory."

Coaching days at Edinburgh ceased in 1846, when that sole surviving relic of the coaches between London and the North—the Edinburgh and Berwick coach— was discontinued on the opening of the Edinburgh and Berwick Company, completing the series of lines that connect the two capitals. It is true that passengers could not yet travel through without changing, for the great bridges that cross the Tyne at Newcastle and the Tweed at Berwick were not opened until four years later ; but it was possible, with these exceptions, to journey the whole distance by train. The opening of the railway meant as great a change for Edinburgh as did the beginning of the New Town seventy years before. Just what it was like then we may judge from the drawing made from the Castle by David Roberts in 1847. The point of view he has chosen is that from the Mons Meg Battery, and the direction of his glance, omitting the Old Town on the right, is to the north-east. Changes in detail have come about since then, but, as a whole, it is the Edinburgh we all know : the Calton Hill, with its cluster of weird monuments, prominent ; the New Town, stretching away vaguely to the water-side ; while in the distance, on the right, is seen the shore curving to Portobello ; the twin masses of the Bass Rock and North Berwick Law on the horizon. Down in the New Town itself the changes are evident. Where the toy train with its old-fashioned locomotive is crawling out of the tunnel under the Mound, and where the old Waverley Station is seen, alterations have been plenty. The old North Bridge pictured here has given place to a new, spanning the ravine in three spans of steel. Beyond it are still seen the smoked-grimed modern Gothic battlements of the Calton Gaol, but the huge new hotel of the North British Railway has replaced the buildings that rose on that side of the old bridge, while the towering offices of the *Scotsman* occupy the other, all in that florid French Renaissance that is the keynote of modern Edinburgh's architectural style. The Scott Monument stands where it did, not, as David Roberts's drawing shows us, among grounds but little cared for, but amid gay parterres and velvet lawns. The Bank of Scotland has been rebuilt and all the vacant sites long built upon ; evidences these of half a century's progress, the direct outcome of those railways that two generations ago wrote " Finis " to the last chapter in the romantic story of the Great North Road.

SKYLINE OF THE OLD TOWN.

INDEX

S

INDEX

Printed in Great Britain
by Amazon